Footlights Across the Border

American University Studies

Series XXVI
Theater Arts

Vol. 1

PETER LANG
New York • Bern • Frankfurt am Main • Paris

Elizabeth C. Ramírez

Footlights Across the Border

A History of Spanish-language Professional Theatre on the Texas Stage

PETER LANG
New York • Bern • Frankfurt am Main • Paris

Library of Congress Cataloging-in-Publication Data

Ramírez, Elizabeth C.
 Footlights across the border : a history of Spanish-
language professional theater on the Texas stage /
Elizabeth C. Ramírez.
 p. cm. — (American university studies.
Series XXVI, Theater arts ; vol. 1)
 Bibliography: p.
 1. Mexican American theater—Texas—History.
2. Mexican American drama (Spanish)—History and
criticism. 3. Mexican Americans—Texas—Intellectual
life. 4. Theater—Texas—History. I. Title. II. Series.
PN2270.M48R36   1990   792'.09764—dc19   88-28585
ISBN 0-8204-1035-7   CIP
ISSN 0899-9880

CIP-Titelaufnahme der Deutschen Bibliothek

Ramírez, Elizabeth C.:
Footlights across the border : a history of Spa-
nish-language professional theatre on the Texas
stage / Elizabeth C. Ramírez. — New York;
Bern; Frankfurt am Main; Paris: Lang, 1990.
 (American University Studies: Ser. 26,
 Theater Arts; Vol. 1)
 ISBN 0-8204-1035-7

NE: American University Studies / 26

Copy of the front page of *La Prensa,* 25 December 1924, San Antonio is courtesy of
The Barker History Center, University of Texas at Austin.

Photographs of Leonardo Astol are courtesy of the private collection of Sra. Otila Garza,
Austin, Texas.

Photographs from the Villalongin Collection are courtesy of the Villalongin Archives, Benson
Latin American Collection, University of Texas at Austin.

© Peter Lang Publishing, Inc., New York 1990

Printed by Weihert-Druck GmbH, Darmstadt, West Germany

To my parents,

Margarita C. & Pedro F.

Ramírez

Table of Contents

Table of Illustrations

Illustration

Table of Illustrations

Preface

This account of the history of Mexican American Professional theatre in Texas was recorded and remembered by people who witnessed those events. Such individuals as Carlos Villalongín and Leonardo F. García left repertories with their distinctive directorial markings, broadsides and programs, and other theatrical memorabilia which until recently sat on bookshelves, in old trunks, and nestled in their children's memoirs of the past. My investigation into the Spanish-language theatre in Texas opened up those almost lost moments in which theatre was at its peak in the booming Mexican American communities within the State. Texas has historically been a land of great promise and wealth and this unfolding of a cultural contribution of Mexican Americans adds to both.

I am indebted to Sra. María Luisa Villalongín de Santos and Sr. Lalo Astol, his wife, Susie, and his eldest daughter, Mrs. Otila Garza, all of whom have provided the missing links and helped to substantiate the information I have gathered.

Fortunately, the University of Texas at Austin provides an ideal setting for pursuing an investigation of Spanish-language activities within the State of Texas through its extensive collection of Spanish-language newspapers and repertory collections of Carlos Villalongín and Lalo Astol.

My indebtedness to individuals, publishers, libraries, and collections for permission to reprint materials is acknowledged in the credits accompanying the illustrations and source materials. Permission to use my article published in *Theatre Survey* was granted by the American Society for Theatre Research through the help of the editor, Roger Herzel. I am also grateful to the Mid-America Theatre Conference, Inc. and Ron Engle for allowing me to use a portion of my article published in *Theatre History Studies*.

Preface

I would like to thank Mario and Pedro Ramírez, my brothers, for their assistance in photographing materials. I owe a personal debt of gratitude to Patricia, William, and Guillermito Ramírez-Long. Above all, I wish to express my gratitude to Jorge Huerta, Ricardo Romo, Julian Olf, John W. Brokaw, and Oscar G. Brockett for their thoughtful reading and helpful suggestions for improving the manuscript.

E.C.R.

American Repertory Theatre
Institute for Advanced Theatre Training
Harvard University
October 1988

Introduction

Mexican theatre predates the first English-speaking theatre on the American continent. It began in the sixteenth century when amateur groups from Mexico initiated religious plays which to this day are performed in what was to become the southwestern United States. Professional companies did not arrive in Texas, however, until the nineteenth century and their activity did not reach its peak until the Mexican Revolution caused so many companies to emigrate to the United States after 1910.

While some historical works have touched on amateur Mexican American drama, no detailed study of the professional Spanish-language theatre in Texas exists. Nevertheless we know that during the late nineteenth century (and perhaps earlier) these professional acting companies arrived in the United States from Mexico and began the tradition which still lives today.[1] The professional companies played a major role in building cultural life in Texas, although their contributions are ignored in current histories. In the latter half of the nineteenth and in the early twentieth century, the largest concentration of Mexican Americans in the United States could be found in Texas. This State offered significant opportunity to Mexican professional acting companies, so, it is high time that we examine them and their contributions.[2]

This study will explore the aspect of Mexican American culture in Texas that is revealed by their theatre and its drama between 1875 and 1935. Despite such difficulties as limited primary evidence, scattered and imprecise secondary materials, and a scarcity of eye-witness accounts of the performances, this study, nevertheless, is based on sufficient evidence to permit a tentative evaluation of a major theatrical current in the southwestern United States.

Chapter I examines the social and cultural environment of Mexico and Texas in the latter half of the nineteenth century in order to establish the setting of the earliest professional Spanish-lan-

guage theatre in Texas. An examination of a representative dramatic company sheds light on its organization and operations prior
to 1900.

Chapter II analyzes the dramas on the Spanish-language stage.
Through these analyses we can discern the tastes and demands of
the Mexican American community, which in turn influenced the
policies and practices of the acting troupes, especially those that
appeared after 1900.

Chapter III examines the acting troupes that appeared between
1900 and 1935. Since three distinct types of companies appeared
on the American stage, it is necessary to analyze the organization,
operations, and contributions of each type by focusing on specific
companies.

Chapter IV deals with production elements and processes; costumes, scenery, lights, and acting. The visual aspects of the production, the acting styles, and particular actors and actresses are discussed and evaluated.

Chapter V focuses on the audience and its response to the actual
performance, and Chapter VI surveys the reasons for the decline
of professional dramatic Spanish-language companies in Texas.

Many terms have been used to designate the Spanish-speaking
people of the southwestern United States: "Spanish," "Mexican,"
"Hispanic," and in the mid-1960s, with the growing desire for separate identity, "Chicano." Chicano is a popular term, synonymous
with Mexican American, adopted in the 1960s by those who were
experiencing an awakening pride in their Mexican ethnicity, while
acknowledging that residency in the United States sets them apart
from those Mexicans living south of the border. As an outgrowth
of the Chicano Movement, the Spanish-language theatrical troupes
that arose in the southwestern United States called themselves
"Chicano Teatros," to indicate that they were both political and cultural in nature and distinct products of their time. Since this study
is an investigation of the origins and development of Spanish-language theatre in Texas, and therefore concerned with a broader
spectrum than would be indicated by "Chicano," I have chosen to

use Mexican American to designate the groups with which I am concerned.

Because most of the information now available is in scattered Spanish sources the principal value of this study lies in its detailed analysis in English of the varying theatrical activities of Mexican Americans. Existing scholarly works in English devoted to this subject include four published articles surveying Mexican American drama in particular areas of the United States.[3] A few articles dealing with dramatic production, touring companies, and brief analyses of twentieth-century plays and performances have also appeared.[4] While these studies are valuable, the time has come to give a comprehensive overview of the professional Mexican American theatre in Texas. What follows here is an an attempt to do just that.

Notes

1. Elizabeth C. Ramírez, "A History of Mexican American Professional Theatre in Texas Prior to 1900," *Theatre Survey* May and November 1983: 99-116. John W. Brokaw, "A Mexican American Acting Company, 1849-1924," *Educational-Theatre Journal* 27 (1975): 23-27.

2. See Ricardo Romo, "The Urbanization of Southwestern Chicanos in the Early Twentieth Century," *New Scholar* 6 (1977): 183-207.

3. John W. Brokaw, "Chicano Theatre: Some Reflections," *Educational Theatre Journal* 29, 4 (December 1977): 535-544. John W. Brokaw, "The Repertory of A Mexican American Theatrical Troupe: 1849-1924," *Latin American Theatre Review* Fall 1974: 25-35. Jorge A. Huerta, "Chicano Agit-Prop: The Early Actos of El Teatro Campesino," *Latin American Theatre Review* 10 (1977): 45-58. Jorge A. Huerta, "Chicano Teatro: A Background," *Aztlán* 2 (1971): 63-78.

4. John W. Brokaw, "A Mexican American Acting Company, 1849-1924." Jorge A. Huerta and John Harrop, "The Agitprop Pilgrimage of Luis Valdez and El Teatro Campesino," *Theatre Quarterly* 5 (1975): 30-39.

Chapter I

Beginnings to 1900[1]

The last quarter of the nineteenth century witnessed the beginning of Mexico's "Golden Age."[2] During this time Mexico received bounteous foreign capital; industry and agriculture flourished; railroads pushed their way south from the United States; the ancient *reales de minas* of the Spaniards reopened, and smelters began to "belch their yellow fumes into the desert air."[3] The valuable silver, gold, copper, lead, and zinc flowed north to feed the rapidly expanding commerce and industry of the United States, and many domestic products found a ready market abroad. The Capital city was cleaned up and modernized, electric lights and streetcars were everywhere, and many new buildings arose, such as the elaborate Palace of Fine Arts. Porfirio Díaz, Mexico's president during these years, surrounded himself with able *científicos*, a group of brilliant lawyers and economists who "worshipped at the new and glittering shrine of Science and Progress" and who as cultivated men brought, along with Mexico's material improvements, cultural ornaments as well.[4] They encouraged poetry, novels, art, and music, all of which thrived in Mexico City. The theatre was just as much a part of that cultural growth as the other arts. Beyond question the economic and cultural development of Mexico during the regime of Don Porfirio was great.

The State of Texas found itself caught up in the growth and prosperity of both Mexico and the United States. Its cultural life was also blossoming, but in an almost unique manner. There were several communities of Germans, Blacks, and other ethnic groups within the State, including two particularly large communities: Mexican American and Anglo American.[5] While the Anglo American community was English-speaking, the Mexican Ameri-

can community remained Spanish-speaking. In spite of this difference, however, both groups participated in and contributed to the
thriving cultural environment of Texas as it developed. Mexican
Americans, like other ethnic groups, had a culture more or less independent from the English-language group. Nowhere was that
independence more evident or important than in the theatre.

Because English and Spanish-speaking communities lay in the
path of a general westward movement which continued with the
growth of towns and expansion of the railroads, both enjoyed a vibrant cultural life. Texans experienced the same major trends in
art, architecture, sculpture and music enjoyed throughout the nation. Much of the popular entertainment from other parts of the
country, such as road shows, circuses, and popular music, also appeared in Texas. Certainly both communities could and did participate in such entertainment without being hindered by language
barriers. Yet it was evident that the Spanish-speaking community
at the same time made a conscious effort to continue traditional
practice and lifestyle. Celebrations and entertainment specifically
for the Spanish-speaking in Texas centered around traditional in-
digenous festivities; bullfights as well as cockfights were also extremely popular, as were evening serenades and concerts in the
plaza. That heritage came from Mexico and, before that, from
Spain. The art and music of Mexican Americans were greatly influenced by both of those countries.

Mexican Americans were able to renew and reinforce their cultural heritage because, while the border between the United States
and Mexico was established in 1848 with the signing of the Treaty
of Guadalupe Hidalgo, prior to 1924 it could be crossed in either
direction at almost any point with the greatest of ease. As Carey
McWilliams reminds us, the Rio Grande does not separate the
people on either side, but rather "draws them together." He continues:

> Along the river, as along the entire border, the towns are twins, and Siamese
> twins, in some cases, for many of them have interconnecting communications
> .... Speaking of the residents of El Paso and Juárez, Walter Prescott Webb

has said that "the river instead of separating them, rescued them from the desert and bound them together; all depended upon it both for domestic purposes and for irrigation. . . ; across its muddy channel the Mexicans intermarried, celebrated the same festivals, observed the same religious rites, rejoiced the same feast days, and shared their sympathies, passions, and prejudices."[6]

The Spanish-speaking population in Texas continued to grow, much of it moving further north and away from the border. In the last quarter of the nineteenth century the total population of Texas was approximately two and a quarter million with Mexican-born numbering about fifty thousand. Because these immigrants sought employment, Mexican Americans were primarily found in urban rather than rural areas; that is where the jobs were.[7] Not all were recent immigrants or poor. They belonged to various social and economic classes. Some were wealthy, educated and cultured individuals. As this population grew, the demand for entertainment and a more select social and cultural environment increased. Owing much to the proximity to Mexico as well as the continual influence from Spain, distinct trends and practices developed to answer that demand.

The growing demands for entertainment and a more select cultural life affected the theatre. It was in the theatre where the separation of the Anglo American and Mexican American communities was evident, since the use of the Spanish language excluded most non-Mexican Americans. Although other ethnic groups also had their theatres in Texas, the Mexican American community was unique in supporting professional dramatic companies on a regular basis. These companies were professional in that they were composed of skilled individuals who were paid for their performances and seem to have derived their livelihood from working full-time with the company. These professional companies, already thriving in Mexico, could be found on the Spanish-language stage in Texas.

The English-speaking theatre had also become more accessible as it expanded westward. Several studies of theatrical activity in Texas show that it was an important and vibrant part of the State's evolving cultural life. The Anglo American theatre, however, was dominated by large touring companies travelling from the East Coast and abroad, generally giving only a few performances in any venue. Only the Mexican American community had resident professional theatre available to it on a regular basis.[8]

Many forms of Spanish-language entertainment, both amateur and professional, flourished within the State. Even before the advent of the professional Spanish-language acting companies in Texas, a lively amateur theatre existed which dates from the seventeenth century. The tradition begun by the first friars in Mexico of educating the natives through religious drama was continued by the Spanish colonists throughout the southwest. One such drama, *Los Pastores* (*The Shepherds*), remains one of the most widely produced Spanish-language religious plays in the southwest. It is difficult to date the first Indo-hispanic version of this and other religious plays. Arthur L. Campa states that because of their being "modelled after the Spanish *autos*," they are "strictly seventeenth century at the earliest."[9] Accounts of amateur productions of the play of the shepherds indicate that it was commonly produced throughout the State.[10]

Information regarding the development of the professional Spanish-language theatre in the United States is sadly lacking; however, we know that during the nineteenth century and perhaps earlier the Spanish-language acting companies that arrived in Texas from Mexico formed a lasting tradition in the United States. This tradition was particularly strong in Texas.

No one knows exactly when the first professional Spanish-language theatrical company appeared in Texas. At least some Mexican American actors had turned "professional" by 1875. Joe Manry, in his study of the theatre in Austin, lists "The Mexican Theatre" as one of the structures available in that city for productions.[11] Nothing is known about the theatre save that it opened in the winter of 1875 near the Colorado River southwest of the courthouse and, while it may not have offered Spanish-language theatrical fare exclusively, it must have specialized in that sort of entertainment. The permanence of the structure suggests that besides visiting Mexican companies, professional Mexican American companies (companies residing in the United States for at least some duration) would have either included this theatre in their tours or performed there as residents of the city.

The earliest professional Spanish-language acting company about which we have evidence appeared in Texas just prior to 3 December 1884, when it performed at the Salón-Teatro del Mercado in Laredo. The two documents regarding this company provide only a few details. We discover, first, that the company was comprised of at least four "distinguished" actors well-known on the Mexican stage;[12] second, that one of the actors, Francisco E. Solórzano, was to become a prominent figure in the development of Mexican American theatre in Texas; third, that possibly an established travel route existed which was used by touring companies from Mexico to Texas; and finally, that the audience was pleased with the actors' performances and the repertory selections.

The importance of this early appearance of Solórzano in Texas cannot be overlooked. He must have acquired some idea of the facilities and potential market for his further enterprise as theatre manager and company director within the State. Before 1900, however, Sr. Solórzano did not remain in Texas permanently. This remarkable actor went on to acquire fame as a theatre manager, company manager, and director in at least two major Mexican theatres before he appeared again on the Texas stage.[13]

We have virtually no indication of the repertory of this company although we know that its bill included a drama and a comic afterpiece. We learn from one account that in this performance the apparently moving drama *El gran Galeoto* (*The Great Galeoto*) by José Echegaray was followed by a humorous afterpiece entitled *Heráclito y Demócrito* (*Heraclitus and Democritus*), in which the two actors demonstrated great skill and ingenuity. This latter piece "helped to somewhat dispel the emotion that the drama had created."[14]

Although some Mexican companies eventually found permanent homes in Texas, this company did not remain in the State. All of the actors named in the accounts of December 1884 continued to be active on the Mexican stage until the end of the century. It was reported that this company had given the Laredo public many "pleasurable moments" and thus we may assume that it had acted there prior to 3 December. The company nevertheless left Laredo to appear in San Antonio, where it was expected to give only two or three performances before returning to Mexico.

Throughout the latter part of the nineteenth century, newspapers announced theatre companies' arrivals in Texas. These accounts, along with available playbills, promptbooks, and private collections of plays and memorabilia of former company members and descendants of actors and actresses show that most were from Mexico, but a few came from Spain. The accounts available reveal that, while occasionally companies produced other genres besides their specialities, most specialized in 1 of 4 forms: opera, operetta, *zarzuela* (Spanish operetta or musical comedy), or drama. The dramatic companies were the most numerous, best documented, and thus the most revealing of audience tastes and theatre practice.[15]

We know that at least eight dramatic troupes performed in Texas and they had much in common with respect to organization, policy, and practice. One such group about which we know rather more than the others provides an interesting case study.

The Compañía Dramática Solsona, typical of others, was composed around a family nucleus, produced only dramas, and toured. When first mentioned in the press, the Compañía Solsona had just arrived in San Diego, Texas, from Laredo at the end of August 1891. Attendance for the first performance on Saturday was poor because of rain, but by 11 September the company was reportedly attracting large audiences and preparing to commemorate the Independence of Mexico on the 15th and 16th of September. It is unknown how long the company remained in San Diego, but by November 1891 it was scheduled to perform at a benefit for a Catholic Church in Corpus Christi at the Altos del Mercado. The company was said to be "always well received" there, which indicates prior performances; it again captured the "sympathies of the entire public" on that occasion. The troupe's abundant coverage in the newspapers indicates a greater popularity than its rivals.[16] The company was reported to be working successfully in San Antonio as of 18 February 1892, and by the end of March it was said to be one of the two Mexican dramatic companies vying for the public's attention.

We do not know how extensive the tours of other Spanish-language companies were although we do have the earlier account of activity in Austin. It seems likely, however, that Mexican travelling companies usually appeared only in the major cities, namely, Laredo, San Antonio, and El Paso, since the railroads had direct routes to these cities and the Spanish-language newspapers in these cities generally made mention of social and cultural events occurring throughout the State. Much of what was announced did not even occur in the city in which the accounts appeared. The appearance of the Compañía Solsona in San Diego and Corpus Christi seems unusual, but we cannot be certain.

The Compañía Solsona had longer runs than other troupes. The company performed every Sunday on a regular basis at the Teatro Salón San Fernando and apparently settled permanently in San Antonio. The *General Directory of the City of San Antonio*, published in 1896, which lists Francisco Solsona (1844-?) as a musician, indicates that he and his wife, Carmen Velasco Solsona (1856-?), resided in San Antonio. The earliest church census also lists five others in the same household. Francisco Solsona was born in Spain, and Carmen and three others were born in Mexico. Violante and María were born in Texas. María was listed as married, but there is no indication of her spouse. It is unclear whether she is a child or a daughter-in-law, possibly married to one of the sons. The fact that the name Solsona appears again in later years in that area supports the assumption that they became permanent residents of that city.[17]

The case of residency is highly significant in this study. Up to the point where we actually can document a company in residence within the State, the Spanish-language troupes can only be viewed as contributors in different ways as tourists in commercial ventures or in some instances as exiles from Mexico.

The management of the company was undertaken by Sr. Francisco Solsona, who was also the director. It was common practice for company managers also to serve as directors, but the fact that at one time the company had two managers and probably two directors as well is unusual. The account of 4 November 1891 mentions that the company was under the name and management of two men, Solsona and González.[18] We do not know who González was or what he did, besides lending his name briefly to the troupe's advertisements, but he appears to have been a partner of and therefore co-manager with Solsona. Unfortunately, the newspaper which provides us with most of the information on this company, *La Fe Católica* of San Antonio, begins in 1898 and the issues available only extend to 1900, at which time the company was still active.

The Solsona company consisted of eight members each in different lines of business, a practice common to all the companies. ("Lines of business" refers to the types of characters that an actor always played, as for example, old men, leading roles, low comedy, and so on.) However, because of the company's smaller size, the actors played a wider range of roles than they would have in a larger one. The lead roles were assigned to Solsona and his wife. Other family members in the company were Pepe or José Solsona (possibly a nephew or cousin), who played juvenile leads (*galán joven*); Srta. María Solsona, generally the ingenue (*dama joven*); and Cuca (a nickname, probably for the youngest daughter), who played little girls. The second-line parts were played by Sr. Vela Montemayor, Sr. Rodríguez, and Srta. María Borel. Sr. Rodríguez, the favorite in many performances, often played opposite Srta. Borel. She was said to be "young and beautiful" and thus may have also alternated in the ingenue roles with María or played soubrettes. Occasionally local amateurs were included to fill in the required roles.[19]

According to available accounts we know that this company performed on Sundays in San Antonio on a regular basis, presenting a different play each week. It is important to note, however, that the accounts are found in a weekly newspaper which appeared only on

Saturdays, and thus the announcements were probably only for events scheduled for the next day. There is no indication of what the company did during the week except that the reporters always mention witnessing the company preparing for their upcoming performances. We cannot dismiss, however, the possibility that the company performed on other nights of the week, perhaps in another theatre in the same city. They may even have toured in surrounding communities throughout the week. Earlier accounts record that the company performed on other days besides Sundays.[20]

The bill was similar to that of the earlier company mentioned in Laredo in that it included a full-length drama followed by a *juguete cómico*, consisting of a short comic play with songs that followed the longer dramas. There are many comic short pieces found in the extant repertory collections of two other companies, the Compañía Hernández-Villalongín and the Compañía Azteca.[21] The evening often concluded with songs from these latter pieces or choruses from popular *zarzuelas* sung by the company members at the request of the audience. The bill was changed every Sunday and the addition of new plays was common. The plays were performed with intermissions between acts, the *entr'acte* entertainments generally consisting of songs rather than comic sketches.[22]

The repertory consisted primarily of romantic and sentimental drama (Spanish), although some works by Mexican dramatists appeared as well. The plays presented by the Compañía were of a moralistic, instructional nature with religious overtones, as evidenced by such titles as *Paula o la nueva adúltera* (*Paula or the New Adultress*), *El angel conciliador* (*The Conciliatory Angel*), and *El esclavo de su culpa* (*The Slave of His Guilt*). The popular dramas *Le conviene esta mujer* (*This Woman Suits Him*) and *Malditas sean las mujeres* (*Damned Be All Women*) also appeared as well as the historical drama *Los mártires de Tacubaya* (*The Martyrs of Tacubaya*).

Generally, the quality of the performance was considered more than adequate, but the newspaper reprimanded the company when it was "not well rehearsed," as was the case on 19 June 1898.[23] The reviewer said that there were reasons to be taken into account for its less than adequate performance, although we do not know what these were; however, apparently even this performance was acceptable to the public. Thus, we get a glimpse of the rapport that began to develop, at least in the larger cities, between newspapers and the acting companies. From this and other accounts we see that the newspapers provided important information to the general public since the companies apparently did not buy advertisements.

Few Texas theatres accommodated Spanish-language touring companies at this time, but certain other buildings served the companies regularly. Performance halls were established by societies and fraternal groups generally for their own activities, and companies used them for performances because the commercial theatres, with other more lucrative bills, were available to them only occasionally. The performance halls, in which facilities of varying kinds were available, were operated by the sponsoring social groups. Such halls were typically located in the center of the Mexican American communities. The Teatro Salón del Mercado in Laredo was the facility most often used by companies that performed in that city, and it was also used for many other attractions, meetings, and social occasions.

Virtually none of these halls nor any plans or photographs remain, yet the Teatro Salón San Fernando was typical and many residents of San Antonio can still recall its prominent features. The Teatro Salón San Fernando operated loosely under the auspices of the Catholic cathedral, but a secular society organized for the benefit and good-will of the Mexican community was the organization in sole charge of its management. The salon, a large hall with a raised stage, had little wing space or backstage area, which indicates limitations on the use of special scenic effects, thus telling us something about the Compañía Solsona's performances. It is probable that this salon accommodated about 200 seats, since that was the capacity of most such facilities.

In regard to theatre management, little is known. The minimal direct advertising that was done--i.e., the distribution of handbills and broadsides--was handled by the company's actors. The theatre managers seem to have had no active role in publicizing the events. Examples of these broadsides or announcements, which generally include the title of the drama as well as the cast list, are available in the Villalongín Collection at the Latin American Collection Library at The University of Texas at Austin. Apparently the theatre managers at this time were required to do little more than provide a space and arrange contracts with the managers of the acting companies. Companies never arrived in a city without having previously made written or verbal arrangements with a theatre manager for a certain number of performances at any facility. Since this was a common practice in Mexico, it may be assumed that similar arrangements were made in Texas.

The general commentary about actors and actresses that appeared in local newspapers stressed that they were well received by the public.[24] Of the members of the Solsona company, it was said that all actors performed satisfactorily and their songs were so pleasing that they were asked to repeat them. Their roles were recognized as "difficult to portray" and the actors succeeded in "making their performances memorable." Especially notable was Sra. Carmen V. Solsona, who was "not only irreproachable" but was able to accomplish a "truly inspired labor" and earned the ovation she received.[25]

In analyzing the audiences and performances it is possible to determine the values of the people at this time. Virtually all theatrical entertainment was given front page coverage in Laredo and El Paso. In San Antonio extensive reviews and commentaries were always found before and after the performances. Given these facts, it is apparent that people in those cities had a strong interest in the theatre and held it in very high esteem. Although these cities still lacked extensive theatrical activity and the troupes were almost always enthusiastically received, the audiences were somewhat discriminating. In an account which appeared in 1891, the performances at the Centro-Salón del Casino de la Vecina Villa in Laredo were said to be in direct contrast to those which were occurring at the "elegant little theatre where the Compañía Hernández is appearing," for "this theatre has an inferior company, poor performances, and has nothing edifying [or instructive] to offer."[26] The didactic element of a performance was considered the most valuable contribution that a play and a company could make. The response of the audience to its absence illustrates the discriminating tastes of the public.

The newspaper *El Correo de Laredo* regarded the Mexican American society of Laredo privileged to see the troupe of Sr. Hernández although that company apparently had only appeared on the Mexican side, Nuevo Laredo. It was hoped that the company would appear on the United States' side of the border, but whether it did or not is unknown. Almost a year later, in March of 1892, the people of Laredo were said to be "like children in limbo" in contrast to San Antonio's inhabitants, who had two dramatic companies competing for their attention.[27] The only mention we have of activities in El Paso is a proposal presented on 18 September 1897 to the Ayuntamiento, the municipal government, in which seventy of the more prominent persons of that city, many of them women, requested by petition that hats with high tops be prohibited from the theatres. Audiences seeking to be entertained and provided with suitable productions under pleasant circumstances had apparently found themselves hindered by boors in large hats.

The accounts in the San Antonio area indicate that the newspapers served to educate the public and the performers on what was proper in the theatre. On 7 May 1898, for example, the newspaper *La Fe Católica* states that it "must censure harshly the discourtesy of some poorly educated people who without proper respect of any sort for the families, interrupted the performances by conversing in loud voices, laughing ridiculously and, what is more incredible, singing each verse during the choruses which even sheep herders would not do."[28] From this account we can already see that the theatre was providing entertainment for families and was required to be appropriate for the many families in attendance. Families, of course, were on both sides of the footlights. It is important to add that the audience members also included some of the most illustrious and select among the "aristocratic Mexican-Texan

society."[29] It was vital that such members of society, many of whom
were "young ladies of society and of distinguished families of both
the Anglo and Mexican community," not be insulted at the theatre
by the poor behavior of some.

Newspapers were also quick to criticize the performers harshly
when they saw something they considered unacceptable. One such
censure of the Solsona company came as a result of the inappropriate singing of the Mexican National Hymn at one performance:

> We sincerely believe that the marching tunes of this hymn of the mother
> country should only be performed at civic celebrations where the nation is
> paying tribute to its heroes. Our National Hymn deserves the highest respect
> and should inspire us with its sanctity and thus it is not a street song but
> rather a patriotic and sublime hymn of our Mother country.[30]

This performance, at least, was viewed as something less than a
"civic celebration"; it is interesting to note, however, the sharp contrast in this case to Mexican theatre practice, where the national
anthem was often sung on stage. Here the reporter considered the
anthem too solemn for such an occasion.

Reviewers were often concerned over the fact that some companies advertised a repertory of "true literary gems" drawn from the
best of the Spanish or Mexican stage, but provided less than adequate performances. In these instances the entire community suffered. The reviewer for the performance at the Casino de la
Vecina Villa stated that the company performing there was
"piteously destroying some works" and "it is all due to one member
who thinks he is notable, but does nothing more than ridicule himself. With such a theatre [the facility was the patio of a tavern
which was sarcastically called "America in Triumph"] and such a
company it is impossible for anyone to attend other than those who
always frequent that place." The severe shortage of theatrical entertainment in the area would still not allow less than quality performances by the companies nor inappropriate performance
places.[31]

Thus from these earliest accounts we can gather some facts
about both audiences and performers from 1875 to 1900. Certainly

both audience and performers were considered to be responsible for appropriate behavior at these theatrical events since not only were families in attendance but also the upper classes of the Mexican and sometimes the Anglo societies. Clearly the theatre provided an important social gathering place and there was a desire to retain it as such for several reasons. The family was the basis for the acting company, its organization and operation, and the audience was composed of families in the same measure, so the fare had to be suitable for everyone. The theatre became a cohesive force in the Mexican American community, a factor most profoundly shown through the church's willingness to sponsor or participate in such activity. The theatre provided a wide variety of fare for the varied audience members and it catered to an unusually wide spectrum of community tastes and values.

The new century would bring many more performers and performances to Texas, filling the annals of American theatre history with a unique tradition. The tastes and demands of the Mexican American community influenced the policy and practice of the acting troupes which soon appeared in large numbers. Thus we can analyze the drama on the Spanish-language stage in order to discover the major characteristics and trends. By studying the plays we will also discover an important aspect of Mexican American theatre in Texas and its place in the culture of Texas.

Notes

1. This chapter has been published in *Theatre Survey* 24 (1983): 99-116.

2. Leslie Byrd Simpson, *Many Mexicos* (Los Angeles: University of California Press, 1969) 294.

3. Simpson 289.

4. Simpson 289.

5. *The Institute of Texas Cultures* (San Antonio: The University of Texas at San Antonio, 1970-1979). A series of pamphlets dealing with the many kinds of people who have contributed to the history and heritage of Texas.

6. Carey McWilliams, *North From Mexico* (New York: Greenwood Press 1968) 59-61.

7. Ricardo Romo, "The Urbanization of Southwestern Chicanos in the Early Twentieth Century," *New Scholar* 6 (2977): 183-207.

8. Joe Manry, "A History of the Theatre in Austin: 1839-1905," diss., University of Texas at Austin, 1979, 1-33, 171-228. Charles Bennet Myler, "A History of the English-Speaking Theatre in San Antonio before 1900," diss., University of Texas at Austin, 1968, 1-13, 346-355. Jack H. Yoacum, "A History of Theatre in Houston: 1836-1954," diss., University of Wisconsin at Madison, 1955, 140. Donald V. Brady, "The Theatre in Early El Paso: 1881-1905," *Southwestern Studies*, 4, No. 1 (1966): 25-39. Ann Taylor Reeves, "Nineteenth Century Theatre in Northeast Texas," M.F.A. thesis, University of Texas at Austin, 1962, 40-92, 177-246. Christa Carvajal, "German Theatre in Central Texas," diss., University of Texas at Austin, 3, 35-36, 57-60, 65-66, 82-85.

9. Arthur L. Campa, *Spanish Religious Folk Theatre in the Southwest, 2nd Cycle* (Albuquerque: University of New Mexico, 1934) 6.

10. *El Correo de Laredo*, Laredo, 9 January 1892: 3.

11. Manry 35, 38.

12. *El Horizonte*, Laredo, 3 December 1884: 2; 6 December 1884: 2. Luis Reyes de la Maza, *El teatro en México con Lerdo y Díaz: 1873-1879* (Mexico: Universidad Nacional Autonoma de México, 1963) 45, 108, 110, 151, 166, 201, 202. Reyes de la Maza, *El teatro en México durante el Porfirismo* (Mexico: Universidad Nacional Autonoma de México, 1965) 12, 67.

13. Manuel Mañon, *Historia del Teatro Principal de México* (Mexico: Editorial "Cultura," 1932) 118, 136. Enrique de Olavarría y Ferrari, *Reseña histórica del teatro en México, 1538-1911*, 5 vols. (Mexico: Editorial Porrua, 1961) 2: 1133 passim.

14. *El Horizonte* 3 December 1884: 2; 6 December 1884: 2.

15. List of companies known to have appeared in Texas arriving from Mexico prior to 1900:

Company Name	Type	Place	Date
Co. Virginia Fábregas	Dramatic	El Paso	23 December 1899
Co. de Opera Infantil	Opera	San Antonio	22 May 1897
Co. de Opera Mendoza	Opera	El Paso	21 October 1899
Co. Roncoroni	Italian Opera & Dramatic	Nuevo Laredo	22 July 1891
		Laredo	5 September 1891
		San Antonio	10 September 1891
		Monterrey	unknown date after 10 September
Co. Rosado	Unknown	El Paso	10 March 1888
Co. with Sr. Solórzano	Dramatic	Laredo	about 3 December 1884
		San Antonio	unknown date after 6 December 1884

Company Name	Type	Place	Date
Co. Dramática Solsona	Dramatic	San Diego	26 August 1891 11 September 1891 15 & 16 September 1891
		San Antonio	February through March 1891 May through July 1898
Co. Solsona y González	Dramatic	Corpus Christi	Before and about 4 November 1891
Co. de Sr. Santos Treviño	Dramatic	Laredo	About 20 September 1891 to 26 September 1891
Co. Valdez	Dramatic	San Antonio	About 31 March 1891
Co. Carlos Villalongín	Dramatic	San Antonio Houston Victoria Dallas	1900 (date unknown)
Cuadro de Operetas Pastoriles	Operetta	Laredo	About 9 January 1892

The following list includes the names of companies that appeared in Mexican cities very near the Texas border and were announced in newspaper accounts as expected to appear in Texas:

Company Name	Type	Place	Date
Co. de Autómatas	"Mechanical actors" [Probably machines or mechanical puppets]	Monterrey	About 15 December 1892
Co. Hernández	Dramatic	Nuevo Laredo	22 July 1981
Co. Opera Italiana	Opera	Monterrey	About 15 December 1892
Co. de Zarzuela de Maestro Ureña	Zarzuela	Monterrey	27 August 1891

Along with extant newspaper accounts, this information is corroborated by the Villalongín Collection and the Lalo Astol Collection in the Mexican

American Collection at the Latin American Library at The University of Texas at Austin; the private collection of Sra. María Luisa Villalongín de Santos, San Antonio, Texas; the private collection of Sra. Otila Garza, Austin, Texas; and interviews with Sra. Villalongín de Santos and Sr. Lalo Astol, San Antonio, Texas, descendants of actors and actresses.

16. *El Correo de Laredo* 26 August 1891: 2; 4 November 1891: 2.

17. *La Fe Católica*, San Antonio, 7 May 1898: 3. The Compañía Solsona had season-ticket holders according to the account of 2 July 1898: 3.
    San Fernando Catholic Church Census, San Antonio Catholic Chancery, San Antonio, Texas. Carmen Velasco Solsona, born in Victoria, Mexico; Amelia Solsona, born 1886, in Durango, Mexico; Arturo Solsona, born 1882, in Nuevo Leon, Mexico; Manuel Solsona, born 1890, in Mexico; Violante Solsona, born 1897, in San Antonio, and María Solsona, born 1881, in Brownsville, Texas.
    General Directory of the City of San Antonio: 1895-1896 (San Antonio: Jules A. Appler, 1896) 543.

18. *El Correo de Laredo* 4 November 1891: 2.

19. The principal lines of business found in a full cast of a Mexican dramatic company would include the following roles: leading actors and actresses (*Primeros actores* and *Primeras actrices*); second-line female (*segunda dama*) and second-line male (*segundo hombre*); character actress (*característica*) and character actor (*actor de caracter*); comic actress (*actriz cómica*) and comic actor (*actor cómico*); young gallant (*galán joven*) and ingenue (*dama joven*). See John W. Brokaw, "A Nineteenth-Century Mexican Acting Company--Teatro de Iturbide: 1856-57," *Latin American Theatre Review* (Fall 1972): 5-18; Luis Reyes de la Maza, *El teatro en México en la epoca de Juárez, 1868-1872* (Mexico: Universidad Nacional Autonoma de México, 1961) 50, 145.

20. *El Correo de Laredo* 26 August 1891: 2; 11 September 1891: 3. The Teatro Salon San Fernando was used for other activities, some of which occurred through the week. See *La Fe Católica* 25 June 1898: 3.

21. The Latin American Library Collection of The University of Texas at Austin has acquired two promptbook collections under the Mexican American Collection project. The repertory of the Compañía Hernández-Villalongín is

listed in the article by John W. Brokaw, "The Repertory of a Mexican-American Theatrical Troupe: 1849-1924," *Latin American Theatre Review* (Fall 1974): 25-26. The collection has been expanded, however, to include 7 more dramas and 4 more one-act pieces. Brokaw's original listing included 146 dramas and one-act pieces.

The Lalo Astol Collection has recently been acquired by the same library. This collection belonged to the Compañía Azteca under the direction of Sr. Astol's father, Leonardo F. García, and includes 39 promptbooks.

22. Some companies only performed the first part of a play on one evening, or one act each evening with subsequent acts through the week. *El Horizonte* 6 December 1884: 2.

23. *La Fe Católica* 25 June 1898: 3.

24. *El Correo de Laredo* 22 July 1898: 3.

25. *La Fe Católica* 21 May 1898: 3; 18 June 1898: 3.

26. *El Correo de Laredo* 22 July 1891: 3.

27. *El Correo de Laredo* 31 March 1892: 2.

28. *La Fe Católica* 7 May 1898: 3.

29. *La Fe Católica* 21 May 1898: 3.

30. *La Fe Católica* 14 May 1898: 3.

31. *El Correo de Laredo* 22 July 1891: 3.

Chapter II

Repertory and Bill, 1900-1935

By 1900 records become more numerous concerning the repertory of the Spanish-language troupes. It was common for newspapers to publish complete lists of the companies' repertories prior to their appearances. Besides there being more newspapers available from this period, there are several extant promptbooks, plays and broadsides in private collections and in the Mexican American Library Collection at the Latin American Library of The University of Texas at Austin.

The drama found on the Mexican American stage in Texas was that found on both the Spanish and Mexican stages. Throughout the history of the Spanish-language theatre in Texas after 1900, the types of plays presented remained the same. Rather than merely listing all the individual plays, we can identify each genre and select representative plays for a more detailed analysis of the drama.

An evening's bill usually consisted of a full-length play and an afterpiece. It must be noted, however, that there were a few exceptions, for occasionally the acts of a drama were presented one at a time on successive evenings until its completion. Infrequent before 1910, this practice was common at the Teatro Aurora in San Antonio. This earlier type of bill was meant to provide a variety of performances and generally included many short comic pieces before and after a single act of a drama along with such other incidental entertainment as songs and dances. The custom of inserting dramatic *entremeses*, dances, and popular songs into the dramatic performances is known to have continued into the early part of the 20th century in Mexico. There are also instances when no afterpiece was offered at all.

More typically, an evening's bill consisted of a long play and an afterpiece. The long plays were serious and the afterpieces generally comic. This arrangement might be changed if the long plays were very serious, when, as one informant states, "out of respect for the play," it was not followed by anything at all. It seems likely that there were also *entr'acte* entertainments, since several notebooks in the extant repertory collections are filled with comic sketches, songs, and other incidental entertainments. There was also always orchestral music at the beginning and between acts and at the end of the full-length plays. (See Broadsides in Appendix I.) Thus, the audience could expect a full and diverse performance for its money.

By 1910 the usual starting time for performances was 9:00 p.m., but by 1915 it was generally 8:30 p.m. Performances lasted between three and four hours, the afterpiece taking as much as an hour of this. Attending the theatre was much in vogue and a variety of ticket prices allowed a variety of social classes to attend. Since it was typical for audiences to emerge from theatres at one o'clock in the morning and sometimes later, we can gather that this form of cultural entertainment provided a safe and secure diversion for its participants.

Bills were changed daily and only occasionally were new plays introduced into the extensive repertories presented by the companies. An account in *La Prensa* shows that for its entire engagement at the Teatro Zaragoza in San Antonio, the resident company performed 57 plays: 17 dramas, two operettas, one major spectacle, and 37 one-act *zarzuelas*. This engagement also included premieres of seven plays (that is, plays which were new in that company's repertory).

The largest number of plays in a company's repertory were comic afterpieces, probably because these were often performed at afternoon "*tandas*," or matinees consisting of a series of short plays, popular for their reduced admission prices. Since even these afternoon bills changed daily, many more comic pieces were necessary.

The two extant repertory collections contain over 160 and 180 plays, respectively. The first collection contains plays mainly by

Spanish dramatists, although some Mexican plays are found as well as French, German, Italian, and Belgian plays in Spanish. (See Appendix II for promptbook titles in both collections not previously published, including divisions by genres, dates, names of authors, and additional comments.)

As to the plays themselves, the plays are primarily serious dramas. There are a few instances of full-length comedies or references to them in advertisements. The term *comedia* is often found, but it is used in the Spanish sense to indicate a full-length play of a serious although not necessarily tragic nature.[1] There are also many *zarzuelas* (or operettas or musical comedies) generally in one act.[2] Most of the plays were produced in Mexico City before the troupes brought them to Texas.

There is enough evidence in the advertisements of troupes to indicate that Texas audiences were exposed to a wide variety of plays, including avant-garde drama which was presented by many troupes almost as soon as it appeared in Mexico City.[3] There are many published lists of companies' repertories indicating the broad range of plays produced and the avid audience interest. Reviews reflect that the public demanded both the old and popular, current productions on the stages of Mexico City, where theatrical activity was centered. Thus, we can gather that the troupes catered to a metropolitan taste in the Texas audiences since the dramas most popular were current productions on the stages in Mexico City.

In the plays themselves, two styles dominate: (1) romantic and (2) realistic. The first, romantic, achieved success in Spain with Angel de Saavedra's (1791-1865) *Don Alvaro or The Force of Destiny*, produced in 1835. Although the success of this play established romanticism in Spain, the vogue was short-lived and declined rapidly after 1840. Among the most important romantic dramatists were Martínez de la Rosa (1787-1862) with *Venice Conspiracy* (1834), Antonio García Gutiérrez (1812-1884) with *The Troubadour* (1836), Mariano José de Larra (1809-1837) with *Macias* (1834), and José Zorrilla (1817-1892) with *Don Juan Tenorio* (1844).[4]

Romanticism arrived in Mexico even earlier than in Spain. The beginnings of romanticism in Mexican drama occur in 1830, although there exists a precursor in José Joaquín Fernández de Lizardi, in whose works the principal features of this style can be found. The major characteristics of his plays are a striving for liberalism and freedom from oppression, issues stemming from the Mexican struggle for independence from Spain. Thus, after the rebellion in 1821, a most favorable climate prevailed in Mexico for the unfolding of romanticism.

Mexico, a collection of regions with frequently changing governments, remained distinctly divided. Historic regional and class distinctions continually plagued unity after it achieved its independence from Spain and from France. The social customs and the spiritual uncertainty in Mexico had encouraged romanticism. While rejecting most things Spanish, due to the desire to free themselves from that country's rule, the Mexican romantic dramatists were greatly influenced by French and German romanticists. Many foreign dramas were adapted and translated. While short-lived in Spain, romanticism remained a dominant style in Mexico throughout the 19th and through the first quarter of the 20th century. The style also dominated the Spanish-language stage in Texas, remaining popular throughout its history.

Another style, realism, which Oscar G. Brockett in his *History of the Theatre* refers to as a "tentative realism," came into vogue in Spain although the transition from one style to the other was evident throughout the period from 1840 to 1875. This style soon appeared on the Mexican stage, popularized especially by two important Spanish dramatists, namely, Ventura de la Vega (1807-1865) and Manuel Tamayo y Baus (1829-1898). Tamayo y Baus' *Love's Madness* (1835) develops the story of Queen Juana's jealousy and *The Positive One* (1862) treats domestic and social problems. Many adaptations of de la Vega's plays and others of this style were written by Mexican dramatists.[5]

The realistic drama in Spain found its first important exponent in José Echegaray (1848-1927), notably in *The Son of Don Juan* (1892), patterned on Ibsen's *Ghosts*, and *The Great Galeoto*(1881), a play about the power of gossip to ruin lives. His *Mariana* (1892) is a social drama written in three acts. For the most part, however, Echegaray's drama was in the romantic vein, in sharp contrast to the realism of the age. He argued that "the sublime in art is in weeping, in pain, and in death."[6] His melodramas revolved around strong passions and sonorous verse, but they also dealt with real social themes.

The war of 1898 resulted in a new movement in literature, "the generation of '98." Jacinto Benavente (1866-1954) was one of the significant dramatists to emerge, composing nearly 300 works ranging through every style and form. *La Malquerida* (*The Passion Flower*, 1913) is perhaps the best known of his realistic plays, dealing with the story of a man's love for his stepdaughter. Popular as they were in Spain, however, realistic plays were generally not produced in Mexico until after 1915. Thereafter, dramatic companies produced realistic works, and some companies became more associated with that style than others. French realists often formed the larger portion of their repertory. Dumas fils, Paul Hervieu, and Alfred Capus are typical examples of dramatists whose works were commonly produced on the Mexican stage.[7]

For the most part, drama primarily remained sentimental and melodramatic amidst some realistic detail. Serafín Álvarez Quintero (1871-1944) and Joaquín Álvarez Quintero (1873-1938), who wrote more than 150 plays of this type, were among the most notable. Similarly, Gregorio Martínez Sierra 1881-1947) wrote *Canción de cuna* (*Cradle Song*, 1911) and *El reino de dios* (*The Kingdom of God*, 1916). Manuel Linares Rivas (1867-1938) wrote *La Garra* (*The Claw*) and *La mala ley* (*The Bad Law*), both written about 1904 and both dealing with the unjust laws forbidding divorce in Spain.

We can gain a clearer and more detailed understanding of the dramas typically found on the Mexican American stages in Texas by examining the major characteristics of representative plays in each of the four primary genres: tragedy, melodrama, serious drama, and comic afterpieces. We can begin with tragedy since this genre represents the earliest type of play produced in the United States by the professional dramatic companies.

Mexican romantic dramas reflect significant Spanish influence through the works of Antonio García Gutiérrez, who wrote *El trovador* (the play on which Verdi based his opera *Il Trovatore*) and many other very successful romantic dramas, and José Zorrilla, creator of *Don Juan Tenorio*. Both of these men were by 1846 considered to be major Spanish romantic dramatists. Furthermore, García Gutiérrez lived in Merida de Yucatán from 1844 to 1849, and Zorrilla lived in Mexico from 1859 to 1866 and was named the director of the Teatro Nacional by the Emperor Maximiliano. Other foreign influences on this type of drama also are evident. The dramas of Hugo, Schiller, and Dumas, just to name a few, were extremely popular on the Mexican stage.[8]

José Peón Contreras' *La hija del rey* (*The Daughter of the King*), a Mexican romantic tragedy written in 1875, was produced often by the Compañía Villalongín. This was a popular piece in the repertory and stands out as a fine representative drama of the romantic style and typical of the tragic genre. Usigli mentions that this play is in Mexico "more than the best of Peón Contreras' personal work, [it is] the best of the Romantic harvest in the nation."[9] The extant promptbook shows that the drama produced was the original drama rather than an adaptation.

The major characteristics of Peón Contreras' drama include: The use of Mexico in the colonial period as the setting; the emphasis on chivalric themes of honor among noblemen, devotion to God, the power of love, passion over reason, and fatality of deception; the conflicts revolving around love, virtue, and honor; and, more importantly, the depiction of Spaniards as tyrants and oppressors, and pessimism about finding happiness and freedom on earth, with hopes of attaining such liberation in Heaven, since death is the only path to eternal glory. There is a desire for nationalism, and an expressed striving for liberalism, indicative of a political movement in Mexico and Latin America.

When one turns to the melodramas in the repertory of the period, it is clear that their popularity is closely linked with political and social struggle in Mexico. Closely resembling the romantic tragedies, the primary distinction between the two genres lies in the use of characters, settings, and situations. Significantly, in the case of melodrama, the plays deal with the common man in familiar circumstances and not, as in the romantic tragedies, with idealized characters in historical settings. The oppression of rustics and lower classes by powerful and wealthy villains is a common theme in melodrama. Their resolution involves the defeat of evil and the triumph of virtue. Clearly, such plays would have an extraordinary appeal to a people striving for honesty and equality in government and society.

There are several significant examples of popular melodramas that reveal this appeal. Among these, *La mujer x* (*Madame X*) was one of the most popular. This drama in four acts and prologue is similar to the story of *East Lynne*, that ever-popular melodrama of the nineteenth century. It presented the heartbreaking suffering of a good but erring woman, and elicited many tears from the audiences. *La madre* (*The Mother*) by Santiago Rusiñol, a Mexican dramatist, is a four-act play in which the erring mother dies at the end of the third act, leaving her honest and good-hearted son who is able to survive wickedness thanks to her. *La garra* (*The Claw*) is another popular melodrama of the period, a two-act play by Manuel Linares Rivas. And finally, the perennial American favorite which was enjoyed around the world, was an attraction in Mexico as well, *La cabaña de Tom* (*Uncle Tom's Cabin*). The version found in the Villalongín collection is dated 1893, and is written in five acts. It was being performed around Monterrey in 1906 by the Compañía Hernández-Villalongín and later in Texas, as evidenced by extant programs of that company.

It is obvious that the melodrama would have an appeal to the Mexican populace. Many of the most popular plays produced in Mexico are again drawn from the repertoire of Spain. The mid-nineteenth century brought to the drama of Spain a reality of daily life reflecting attitudes, customs, and problems characteristic of Spanish society. There was a search for objective presentation of the social ambience to which the hero fits easily. The hero in such plays, unlike his counterpart in romantic drama, is able to resolve the conflict with the established system and is integrated into the new social order. It is such elements as these that are found in *Tierra baja* (*The Lowlands*), a melodrama so long-lived in its popularity on the Mexican American stage that it can serve to illustrate the tastes of those audiences.

Tierra baja, a Spanish play by Angel Guimerá, was written before 1900. It was translated from the Catalán by José Echegaray, one of the most popular dramatists on Mexican and Texas stages throughout the period under study.[10] The major characteristics of Angel Guimerá's play are the use of a rustic setting; the struggle between the oppressor and the common man, illustrating man's desire for freedom and justice; an exaltation of the common man; and the message that, regardless of the most dire circumstances, goodness and virtue always prevail and trust in God leads to happiness. Immediately, the values, beliefs, and aspirations found in this play show evidence of the Mexican American experience in Texas.

The values most evident in this play are illustrated by the people's desire to please God on earth by working hard so that they may attain freedom by owning their own land. Their ultimate belief is that God rules justly over a just universe and hence their circumstances are as good or as severe as they have merited from Him. They aspire to own their own land, but can only attain it by fighting against the oppressor. However, only a select few are willing to go against the oppressor. It is not until Manelich fights and kills the oppressor that some hope of happiness is revealed. While this event gives a sense of optimism for the townspeople, Manelich and Marta seek a complete escape to an ideal happiness by fleeing to the peaceful, beautiful mountains from which the hero had originally emerged. The "high lands" offer the closest place to heaven on earth, and they flee the lowlands forever.

Tierra baja is written in three acts; the first act has eleven short scenes, the second has ten, and the last has twelve. New characters enter during many of the scenes although some scenes are divided as French scenes and begin or end with the arrival or departure of a character. There is unity of place but not of time, with many events occurring in the single setting used in all of the three acts.

The plot begins when Marta, an orphaned girl whose mother is forced to sell her because of her poverty, has been bought by Sebastián, a wealthy landowner. He has stealthily been having sexual relations with the young girl. Because people have begun to gossip and because he is planning to marry another woman for her wealth, he must get Marta out of the way. In an attempt to stop the scandalous gossip that may ruin his own plans for marriage, he has arranged for Marta to be married. He has selected a common, good-hearted, backwoodsman who also lives on his property. This backwoodsman, Manelich, has never seen a woman and immediately falls in love with Marta. The plot mixes serious with comic elements (such as Manelich's love for his goat).

Manelich's goodness and kindness make Marta fall in love with him as well. When Sebastián returns to try to take Marta as his possession again, Manelich fights back. He justifiably kills Sebastián and flees from the lowlands with Marta in search of the hope and promise that awaits them in the highlands. We learn that it is the "tierra baja" (or lowlands in which the common, poor people live) that has prevented its inhabitants from achieving whatever happiness life could have offered them. Their circumstances cannot change for their environment has determined their situation and they have failed to fight back as Manelich has done.

In *Tierra baja*, the characters change. The virtuous and honest Manelich proves he is powerful and can fight the mean and powerful Sebastián. At the end of the play Manelich has completely changed from the manner in which he is first presented. Marta, who wishes only to continue her affair with Sebastián and only feigns love for the woodsman in order to stop gossip in the town, also changes radically as she learns to love this simple, loving sheepherder. She is to be pitied, for she shows what a good and virtuous woman she wishes to be if only her circumstances were different. Ultimately she is admired, for these circumstances are revealed to have been outside of her control. We learn that dire circumstances dictated her loss of virtue and her character is eventually restored through her relationship with Manelich. She then exemplifies all the goodness we see in him.

In *Tierra baja*, as in most of his plays, Echegaray is careful to note precisely how each of the required dialects should be spoken. The drama is written in prose and each character speaks a language appropriate to his background and region of birth. Many declamatory speeches are found throughout the drama, and the dialogue among major characters is eloquent but not as high-flown as in tragedy. As in most of the melodramas, there are many lengthy monologues.

The type of language spoken by the central characters illustrates a more familiar, less poetic quality, along with the "embasticimiento" (or distortion of correct pronunciation) indicated by the dramatist. But it is the hero, Manelich, who most often displays the lack of poetic grandeur in speech as he not only distorts pronunciation but also lacks that power of visualization commonly found among the idealized heroes of the tragic romantic dramas. The following is taken from a description by Manelich of one of his many heroic deeds in the wilderness of Sebastián's land, where he has fought against a wolf that is after his sheep:

> De pronto siento ruido, pisadas, y veo un bulto negro que, dando un bote como un demonio, pasa por encima de mí, resoplando tan fuerte, que sentí el resoplido aquí en el cuello. Los pelos se me pusieron de punta, y por dentro del pecho sentía unos golpes... ¡pum! ¡pum! ¡pum! que me ahogaba. (Soon I feel a sound, footsteps, and I see a black shadow, appearing like a demon, passing over me, breathing so heavily that I felt his breath on my neck. My hair stood on end, and I could feel such a beating inside... thump! thump! thump! that I almost stopped breathing.)[11]

Even when Manelich and Marta are expressing their love for each other and reach moments of high passion, the dialogue reveals the speech of a simple, kind-hearted and common man:

> Yo te quiero, no se por qué. Será porque me has engañado, ó porque he sentido el calor de tu sangre.... Yo no quiero más que besarate, morderte, tan hondo, que la mordedura te llegue hasta el alma. ¡Y apretarte en mis

brazos con afan tan rabiosa, que la vida se confunda con la muerte! Como hombre y fiera. ¡Hombre y fiera, todo junto! ¡Y contigo y contra tí, y contra todos los de la tierra! (I love you and I do not know why. It may be that you trapped me or because I have felt the warmth of your blood. . . . I want nothing more than to kiss you, bite you, so deeply, that the bite will reach your soul. And squeeze you in my arms with such desire that life will fuse with death! Like a man and a beast. Man and beast, both as one! With you or against you, and the opposition of all the earth! [I will continue to love you.][12]

And finally, some of the preface notations of the dramatist concerning the dialogue include: *pa* for *para*; all endings of *ido* changed to *ío* and *ida* to *ía*; and all endings in *ado* changed to *áo*. All of these show that the audiences were receptive to slang and were beginning to hear a more colloquial Spanish--removed from the very formal Castilian Spanish heretofore considered appropriate.

The visual and aural elements in *Tierra baja* demand a realistic set. The dramatist devotes much attention to the detail of furniture and properties to show the appropriate environment that is essential to the story. The setting includes a house interior with several entrances and a large, covered entranceway to the mill area which is surrounded by trees and rocks in the background. Required properties for a mill are visible, such as bags of wheat and tools and other equipment. The setting remains the same for each of the three acts. Throughout the first act, the mill workers in the wheat field are involved in the detailed work of their trade as the action progresses. Activities include groups of peasants singing and dancing in festive dress, as in the scene where the celebration of the nuptials of Manelich and Marta occurs, or people gathered at the mill nearby. Costumes are appropriate to the period and characters. María Guerrero and Fernando Díaz de Mendoza who premiered this production in Spain set the standard. A newspaper clipping showing Díaz de Mendoza as Manelich is found in the "Memoirs of Carlos Villalongín." This photograph shows the sheepherder in typical late nineteenth and early twentieth century dress.

When we turn to serious drama we find that it was quite extensively produced on the Mexican American stage. It runs the gamut from social and historic, to the unique drama of customs of which the work by the Álvarez Quintero brothers is typical. John W. Brokaw notes in his study of the repertory of the Compañía Hernández-Villalongín, that one distinctly Mexican element in this repertory is the patriotic drama. Other private collections of plays also indicate that this type of play was widely used. *Benito Juárez*, a three act verse play, includes 18 characters as well as large crowds. It is an allegory in which one character, "La Patria" or "the mother country," is draped with the Mexican flag. The play simply presents and celebrates Benito Juárez as the hero of Mexico. The tone of the play, as is typical of allegories, is solemn and serious throughout.

The typical qualities of the serious plays include the following: all deal primarily with the family unit and revolve around a conflict that ruptures or threatens the family; they reflect beliefs, values, and aspirations common to Spanish-speaking people; they occur in contemporary Spanish and Mexican settings; they use a wide variety of Spanish to reflect distinct social classes and regional dialects; they reflect through the characters many distinctly Spanish and Mexican customs and manners; all are written in prose; and they intermingle the serious with the comic.

Many more Mexican dramas appear in this serious drama genre than in the rest although Spanish dramatists are liberally represented. It is this type of play that the first native Mexican American dramatists wrote and adapted once they settled in Texas. One such example is *Sangre de Artista* (*An Artist's Blood*), a drama in two acts and in prose, arranged by Leonardo F. García, the director of the Compañía Azteca, who adapted the play from Ventura de la Vega's *La mujer de un artista* (*The Artist's Woman*). Earlier performances by other companies occurred, but it is significant to note that García's script, dated 1932, indicates that it was premiered in San Antonio. This story deals with a painter who feels that he is socially inferior to his wife. She had once been a famous actress and returns to the stage only to earn sufficient funds to pay a famous surgeon to operate on her husband who is losing his eyesight. Their servants provide a number of comic elements in the play. The emphasis here is on typical class discrimination and its potentially destructive effects. Comedy, however, was not merely spice for tragedy; it was an important genre in its own right.

The Álvarez Quinteros contributed to the development of a Spanish comedy of manners and in the process created a new type of regional Spanish drama. These dramatists were greatly influenced by Andalusia, where they lived and wrote. This serious drama has been called "essentially and formally the most representative of Spanish drama of the time."[13] Carefully selected realism was the special characteristic in this regional drama. While Benavente was writing about foreign norms and the decadence and disorientation of the Spanish theatre of the 1890's, the Álvarez Quintero brothers looked into their own past, selected traditions, and illuminated them.

Although there are many popular serious dramas, *El genio alegre* (*The Happy Heart*, 1906) by the Álvarez Quintero brothers of Spain can be viewed as typical of the form. Most of their work was commonly performed in Texas and they remained extremely popular throughout the first quarter of the twentieth century. We can learn much about this type of drama by examining the major features of *El genio alegre*.[14]

In *El genio alegre* the Álvarez Quinteros demonstrate that the worst sinner can be converted by the pure and innocent, and Catholicism is the basis of all successful social and spiritual activity. The values evident in the drama include the following: social change is inevitable and for the best; while class distinctions are useful, they are occasionally cruel, unnecessary, and cause needless conflict among people; the family unit is the basis for peaceful life; and regardless of the measures required, family integrity must be maintained. Despite these rather serious values, the drama is light in tone and we always have the sense that the conflicts are not serious and will eventually be resolved.

El genio alegre shows characteristics that reflect beliefs widely held in Spain. In this play, the concept of honor still dominates this

Spanish society as it had in the Golden Age; the environment determines behavior and manners; the expected behavior and manners of each character play a primary part in the play in terms of class and the role of the individual in society; and the importance of the family unit is revealed.

As a consequence of these beliefs, culture among Texas Mexicans, as reflected in this play, has two features which deserve attention. These features are the principal preoccupations in the work of the Álvarez Quinteros, namely, the importance of home life and the role of women in this society. Through these features many customs that prevailed throughout Spain are illuminated: the custom of religious worship, master-servant relationships, preparation for the "tertulia" (evening gathering for entertainment or intellectual conversations), and the gathering in the patio. These are found to a greater or lesser extent in most of the plays of the Álvarez Quinteros.

The life that the Álvarez Quinteros depict differs strikingly from the realism of Zola in that they do not show what is disagreeable or unpleasant. Manuel Bueno states that the Álvarez Quinteros fulfilled their destiny in making the somber people of the nation laugh, giving this play as the principal cause.[15] The most striking difference is the optimism that pervades the play as these writers depict a life of high spirit, good fortune, and happiness rather than one of misery. Thus we glimpse the values, beliefs, and aspirations in such dramas presented to the Mexican American audiences in Texas.

While full-length comedies are rare in the repertories of the Mexican acting companies, comic afterpieces were included in the repertories. These are generally one-act plays which are quite distinct in many ways from the longer, serious plays. One of the most popular writers of this form is Miguel Echegaray, the brother of José. His plays were very popular, but none more than *Echar la llave* (*Lock the Door*, 1902), a one-act comedy, which deals with such typical themes as deception in marriage, the need to protect one's honor, and the reputation of a virtuous woman placed in doubt. Intrigues, complications, and chance discoveries are common, and the plays typically require fewer characters than those in the other genres discussed.

Comic afterpieces have often been called uniquely Spanish in origin.[16] These were born from the long tradition of Spanish short comic pieces interspersed between acts of longer plays. Hence, the traditions of *pasos*, *entremeses*, and *sainetes*, so popular and long-lived in Spanish drama, are continued by the *"juguetes cómicos"* or comic afterpieces and the one-act *zarzuela* is the most typical. In this genre, that came to be called the *género chico*, are found common stereotypical characters and themes of Spain and later of Mexico. Of course, the most common character types can be traced all the way back to Roman comedies--those of Terence and Plautus--as well as *commedia dell'arte* characters, namely, the *"fresco"* or "fresh" flirt, the *"bruto"* or bully, and the *"tonto"* or dummy. At their side are found the ingenue (*dama joven*) and young gallant (*galán joven*). In all of these pieces are found such general characteristics of comic pieces as misunderstandings, mistaken identities, deliberate deception, double plots, all generally revolving around problems of lovers and parent-child relationships. Typical staging features are the simple setting composed of a single backdrop to indicate a very generalized street scene, the use of music to accompany the comic effects, and the costumes of everyday life conventionalized according to social class, occupation, age, and sex.[17]

This particular genre, however, unlike those already discussed, stands out as uniquely Spanish in origin but reflects both Spanish and Mexican features especially with regard to the following: nationalistic titles, settings, music, and circumstances; character types; customs and beliefs; special theatrical effects; and colloquial speech. Since this genre was popular in both Spain and Mexico, with works being written by dramatists in both countries, these features illustrate the reality of everyday existence that is common in either Spain or Mexico, respectively. Their originality is evident in such titles as *Los granujas*, a name typically given to street waifs (See Illustration I.); *El oro y el moro* (*The Gold and the Moor*); *El sueño dorado* (*The Gilded Sleep*); *La viejecita*, the old lady, whose appearances and dialogue are dependent on her regional dress of the period (See Illustration II.); *La trompa de Eustaquio* (*Eustaquio's Nose*), a play on words which also means "The Eustachian Tube"); and *Mari-Juana*, both a woman's name and the name of a narcotic plant. Other titles include: *El chiflado* (*The Flirt*) and *Mas vale maña que fuerza* (*Wit Over Strength*), which revolves around a popular phrase. All of these titles are distinctly regional although the action can be easily understood in other Spanish-speaking areas as well. The dialogue generally involves a play on words with many Spanish connotations which often refer to a play's title. Thus, adequate translation is almost impossible. The popular language of the masses creates the comic situation in the pieces. Many make extensive use of regional music. Some common customs and beliefs also surface: religious figures and the clergy bear the brunt of jokes and ridicule; gossipy females gather in the patio, marketplaces or *mercados* with individual booths where the owners sell regional foods and drinks; and ghosts and spirits reveal superstitious beliefs. Finally, the names of the characters themselves reflect the types they represent. All of these features can be found to some extent in the representative work chosen here for analysis, *El globo terraqueo.*

One uniquely popular comic afterpiece, *El globo terraqueo* (*The Terraced Haven*, 1904), is a one-act lyrical piece generally referred to as a *zarzuela* on the Mexican stage. Written by Rafael Medina with Manuel Adams of Mexico, it is dated 1904 in the Villalongín Collection, although it was probably produced earlier. This play remained popular throughout the period.[18]

The title of the play, *El globo terraqueo*, illustrates that the author wishes to entertain the audience by blending mix-ups, exaggerations, unusual circumstances, and much confusion. The play shows that procrastination may lead to the unexpected. It also illustrates the belief that an arranged marriage, not for love but for money, generally leads to chaos and unpleasant results; that it is best that parents, in-laws, or others not get involved with other people's affairs of the heart. Moreover, it shows that one seeks to retain one's honor in spite of the ridiculous circumstances in which one may find oneself. The play also reflects the people's superstitious beliefs in ghosts and the bad luck that befalls anyone who walks through the cemetery at night, which in turn illuminates the strong beliefs in Catholic practice, such as invoking saints and the Virgin for protection, making the sign of the cross, and use of the rosary and holy water.

The play seems to be a variation of Feydeau's *Hotel Paradiso*. The plot of *El globo terraqueo* is complex, but incidents occur in such a way that they can be anticipated by the audience. The action is fast and involves much complication and mix-up of characters, places, and situations. The climax occurs in the dark where lovers have arranged to meet out of sight of the over-protective mother and gossipy tenants of the hotel, "El Globo Terraqueo." The action is quickly resolved after a candle is lit and reveals the mix-ups that have occurred in the dark.

All of the scenes occur in front of a painted backdrop of the hotel interior with the generalized street scene visible through the wide front windows. The required furniture and scenic units are portable and placed in front of the backdrop. The audience is always aware of what is going on although the characters themselves are not and there are many surprise encounters as the action unfolds. The unity of time is maintained since the entire play occurs within a single night.

There are eight characters in this short play. It seems unlikely that double-casting could have occurred since all characters appear in either the same scene or immediately afterward in this fast-paced comedy. Although the number of characters is larger than usual, the characters themselves are typical of the form. The characters are of the lower middle class and are always on the look-out for a means of increasing their income. The name of Doña Simona, the owner of the hotel, comes from the "simony" or the fraudulent buying or selling, and can only be topped in its irony by her surnames, "Buitron y Bombardillo." These appellations invoke the images of both a "snare" and a "bomb-vessel" which are implied in the name of a woman who is out to marry her daughter off to the best catch she can find. The daughter, Piedad or "pity," on the other hand, invokes images of a pitiful soul that is not much of a bargain. Doña Poncianita is the proverbial nosy *comadre* or companion to Doña Simona, who wants to be in the middle of all conversations but can neither hear well nor get things straight. Teresa is the servant who is more knowledgeable of home affairs and other matters than the rest and never quite realizes her proper station requires that she be seen but not heard. There is Odon, who is hump-backed and whose name implies "molar" or "a toothache." Finally, there is Don Modesto Canseco, the modest man off the streets who is forever hungry and thirsty and exaggerates everything, including his suffering, his amours, and his sad circumstances since childhood.

The setting is described as the following:

> A dining room of an inn with three to a room. Two doors on each side of the stage. On one side a sofa and on the other two chairs. Each of the four doors has a room number on it. There is a trunk on one side with old pictures and memorabilia. Covered lamps and a kerosene lamp.[19]

The specified doors are required to accomplish the mix-ups at the core of this play. The lighting is of optimum importance since it is in relative darkness that the mix-ups occur, but these must still be visible enough to the audience. French farce obviously influenced this play, yet the setting indicates that it occurs specifically in Mexico. The walls of the hotel visible to the audience should be covered with local commercial announcements, and the hotel's sign indicates that it is located in a small town close to Mexico City. The use of a local newspaper required for the initial scene also aids in establishing the locale.

Aural effects play a vital role. This comic piece, called a lyric play, has music by Curti, a popular Mexican arranger. Music is used to heighten comic business such as setting the suspenseful scene for the arrival of the supposed ghost in the middle of the night. This mood is also created by the sound of bells at key moments.

El globo terraqueo, like most comic pieces of its genre, makes great use of familiar and popular language. Most of these plays are written in prose and the language is often slang with many mix-ups of words. It is most often the misunderstood dialogue which creates the comic situations. The following are just two examples of such mix-ups:

> Luis: ¿Tu sabes quien es calvo? (Do you know who Calvo is?)
> Piedad: ¿El que le falta el pelo? (Someone who is bald?)
> Luis: No, mujer, si pregunto si sabes ¿quien es Lorenzo Calvo? (No, woman, I'm asking if you know who Lorenzo Calvo is?)[20]

She confuses "calvo," which is the term for "bald," with a surname. Later, another character, Modesto, speaks a long soliloquy in which he tells of his past adventures: "Me enamore de ella perdidamente, la quite del caballo, la metí en un coche... ¡y que coche! digo, que noche.... (I fell in love with her so completely that I took her off her horse, put her in the car... and what a car! that is, what a night.)[21] The words "coche" and "noche" sound alike and on using one instead of the other, one implies that the car was more memorable rather than the night or the woman.

Several conclusions can be drawn from this examination of the representative types of plays typically found in the repertories of the Mexican acting companies that appeared in Texas. The dramas of the latter half of the nineteenth century include features that were already prevalent in European drama. Emilio Carilla points out that plays by Dumas, Hugo, and Schiller, as well as by all the major Spanish romantic dramatists, were already being presented on the Mexican stage by the time the principal Mexican dramatists Ignacio Rodríguez Galván and Fernando Calderón began writing. Thus, such familiar features as sentimentalism, abundance of entanglements, frustrated loves, orphans and abandoned honest women were useful in the creation of a Mexican romanticism. In form, the plays ran the gamut from tragedy to melodrama. Fatalism, adverse destiny, and gloom, as well as exaggerated passions, made up the scheme of all the works. Women are exalted and noble sentiments are expressed. The heroes are always chivalrous. Nature is reflected in the plot: there is sunshine or gloom, depending on the state of the souls of the characters. There exists a certain element of mystery and shadiness in some characters. The appeal made in the dramas is not to the mind of the protagonist but to his sensibility and heart. Language is affected, declamatory, and emphatic. All the tragic dramas produced by these companies were historical in content.[22]

Some characteristics are primary in Mexican romantic drama as a whole. Before anything else, the dramas of the Mexican romanticists uphold freedom as the highest ideal. Next to this basic idea of liberty, they advocate patriotism and Christianity. Secondary characteristics include individualism through which the ideal of human justice is exalted. There is also melancholy and sentimentality, but even more so there is a strong sense of pessimism about earthly happiness. Environment reflects rather than motivates mood and action. With regard to form, again freedom is of the essence. There is a mingling of the comic and the tragic, humor with pathos. There is freedom in language, style, and in meter, and glaring improbability of plot.

Magaña-Esquivel has described Mexican romanticism as having "more impatience, melancholy, disillusionment about the outside world, and desire for freedom than existed in other countries."[23] Willis Knapp Jones, in *Behind Spanish American Footlights*, points out that Magaña-Esquivel sees Mexican romanticism as a "synonym of liberalism."[24] Mexican audiences never lost their taste for plays of this type, such as José Zorrilla's *Don Juan Tenorio* which continued to be performed long after Mexican American troupes ceased performing in Texas, as well as other works of both Spanish and Mexican dramatists. The combined efforts of all the dramatists of this romantic movement to educate the audience about the evils of tyrannical rule and the possibilities of loss of freedom remained basic themes on the Mexican stage until the end of the nineteenth century.

The conclusions that can be drawn from studying the plays by the Álvarez Quinteros and the principal female characters in their work are that they reflect a portion of Spanish life of the times. These dramatists depict and investigate customs and beliefs as well as show a changing society. This work is representative of early twentieth century Spanish realistic drama which held the Mexican American stage until the demise of touring and resident Spanish-language dramatic companies.

Finally, the ever popular short, comic pieces illustrate the minor demands required for their staging, the audience's desire for humor as evidenced by the great number of such plays, the acceptance of a changing language, and finally, the popularity of plays reflecting regionalism and kinship with Mexico as the mother country. This genre was at its height in popularity in Mexico during the first quarter of the twentieth century. It was also the basis for the later "sketch" and comic routines which brought vaudeville and variety acts into vogue in the 1920s.

The themes and ideas found in each of the examples of representative dramas reveal the values, beliefs, and aspirations of the Mexican American audiences; that is, their culture and tastes. Audiences valued the use of the Spanish language in varying forms. The Spanish and Mexican settings, both historical and contemporary, indicate the strong sense of nationalism and patriotism in the spectators for their heritage. They believed in the family unit and extolled Catholicism, and while the serious tone of these matters generally prevails, their light and humorous aspects are enjoyed as well. Above all, the people's desire for freedom, happiness, and a better life contributed to the popularity of many of the plays produced for a very long time.

The period between 1900 and 1935 brought to the Texas stage a wide variety of drama produced by a large number of companies. Through the performances the audiences became acquainted with the dramas of international acclaim, from the old and established plays to the modern repertory, both building and influencing the cultural life in America. The Mexican theatre was an elite institution, but the Mexican American theatre catered to all classes. Immigrants stood together, holding on to their heritage, language and traditions as well as adapting to new surroundings and integrating in a new society. The theatre opened its doors to all interested participants, and the Texans gave it a warm reception.

Several individual performers and performances were to make important contributions to American theatre and, as a movement, the Spanish-language dramatic companies were instrumental in introducing and popularizing new ideas and practices. We can now turn to the particular types of companies to investigate their contributions.

Notes

1. *Comedia* is the term used prior to 1700 in Spain to describe any full-length play, whether serious or comic; most were divided into three acts, for the five-act form was never widely adopted in Spain. See Oscar G. Brockett, *History of the Theatre*, 3rd ed. (Boston: Allyn and Bacon, Inc., 1977) 197.

   There is an extensive discussion of the *comedia*, its development and staging in N.D. Shergold, *A History of the Spanish Stage from Medieval Times until the End of the Seventeenth Century* (Oxford: Clarendon Press, 1967). See Chapters 6 and 8, and p. 556.

2. There are many studies available on the Spanish *zarzuelas* and the *género chico*. An analysis of the more popular comic pieces may be found in: José Deleito y Piñuela, *Origen y apogeo del "género chico"* (Madrid: Revista de Occidente, 1949).

3. John W. Brokaw, "A Mexican American Acting Company: 1849-1924," *Educational Theatre Journal* 27 (1975) 28.

4. Brockett 385-386.

5. Brockett 440, 441.

6. Diego Marín, *La civilización española* (New York: Holt, Rinehart and Winston, Inc., 1961) 224.

7. Rodolfo Usigli, *Mexico in the Theatre*, Trans. Wilder P. Scott (University of Mississippi: Romance Monographs, Inc., 1975) 18: 93.

8. Usigli 110-111, Marín 224-225.

9. Usigli 86.

10. Angel Guimerá, *Tierra baja*, trans. José Echegaray, 2nd ed. (Madrid: R. Velasco, Imprenta, 1900).

11. Echegaray 32.

12. Echegaray 56.

13. Richard E. Chandler, *A New History of Spanish Literature* (Baton Rouge: Louisiana State University Press, 1961) 151.

14. Serafín and Joaquín Álvarez Quintero, *El genio alegre*, 2nd ed. (Madrid: Sociedad de Autores Españoles, 1908).
    A copy is found in the private collection of Sra. Otila Garza, Austin, Texas. The roles of Consolación and Julio, the ingenue and young gallant, were played by María Guerrero (1868-1928) and her husband, Fernando Díaz de Mendoza (1862-1930), in the Buenos Aires premiere. The roles are two of many roles which were written specifically for these famous performers. Sra. Guerrero was 38 years old at the time.

15. Manuel Bueno, *Teatro español contemporaneo* (Madrid: Biblioteca Renascimiento, 1909) 120.

16. Alfredo de la Guardia, *El teatro contemporaneo* (Buenos Aires: Editorial Schapire, 1945) 362-369. Deleito y Piñuela 1-50.

17. Oscar G. Brockett, *The Theatre: An Introduction*, 3rd ed. (New York: Holt, Rinehart and Winston, Inc., 1974) 104-109.

18. Interview with Sra. María Luisa Villalongín de Santos, San Antonio, Texas, 1981, Sr. Lalo Astol, San Antonio, Texas, 1981.
    Rafael Medina with Manuel Adams, *El globo terraqueo*. While a copy of this play is available in the Villalongín Collection, dated 1904, I have used the promptbook of Carlos Villalongín from the private collection of Sra. María Luisa Villalongín de Santos. (This promptbook has pages numbered only on the right hand side and thus are indicated either right or left.) Francisco Monterde, *Bibliografía del teatro en México* (New York: Burt Franklin, 1970), dates it at 1905, but the script in the private collection of Sra. Villalongín de Santos indicates that it was copied from a script which premiered at Teatro Principal, Mexico City, on 22 August 1903.

19. *El globo terraqueo* 38 left.

20. *El globo terraqueo* 40 right.

21. *El globo terraqueo* 52 left.

22. Emilio Carrilla, *El romanticismo en el América Hispánica* (Madrid: Editorial Gredos, 1975) II: 47-48.

23. Antonio Magaña-Esquivel, *Breve Historia del Teatro Mexicano* (Mexico City: Ediciones de Andrea, 1958) 66-67.

24. Willis Knapp Jones, *Behind Spanish American Footlights* (Austin: The University of Texas Press, 1966) 482.

Chapter III

The Acting Companies

New York was the main theatrical center in the United States with the road show the usual source of theatrical entertainment in America. The "Theatrical Syndicate" was in forceful control of the American theatre. It was in a position to influence the selection of plays, refusing to accept works that did not appeal to a broad audience and preferring productions that featured stars. Consequently, the American theatre became largely a commercial venture.[1]

Westward expansion of the professional theatre was facilitated by improvements in transportation and the establishment of theatrical centers. The growing population on both the east coast and west led to a demand for theatrical entertainment resulting in enlarged theatres, an increased number of weekly performances, and an establishment of companies and circuits. The theatre flourished as the westward movement accelerated. Journeys were difficult, whether by land or by sea, yet stars visited the new territory almost immediately. Eventually resident stock companies were undermined by starring engagements offering quality performances that were preferred over local troupes. In Texas, several of the theatres in the more largely populated cities became part of the Syndicate's circuit, offering many main attractions that derived from the New York stage.

In Mexico, Mexico City also served as the theatrical center very much as did New York City although no known syndicate or circuit ever existed. However, theatrical activity was not confined to the Capital. It also thrived in the provinces. The provinces were especially important as theatrical centers. Touring companies set out from Mexico City to areas of large population that included Torreon, Monterrey, and Matamoros en route north to Nuevo

Laredo and eventually crossing the border into Laredo, Texas and further afield.

Mexico City not only supported thriving companies but supplied the provinces with many of its most prominent actors. The theatre in the provinces prospered in part because Mexico City kept these theatres supplied with companies and because there was an ever-increasing demand for their performances further and further north as population centers grew. Mexico City served as the training ground for many provincial actors, and it offered a steady supply of new talent to provincial companies. Together, the provincial troupes provided entertainment for virtually the whole of the Spanish-language Texas stage although visiting stars touring infrequently also made significant contributions. Spanish-language professional theatre provided a significant contribution to the culture of the State of Texas.

During the first decade of the twentieth century, the *género chico* (comic short pieces and musical one-act plays) and *zarzuelas* (musical full-length and short plays) became increasingly popular theatrical fare on the Mexican stage. Evidence shows that in Mexico, the number of dramatic actors and companies performing serious drama was large. Few of these actors were able to compete with the companies offering the more popular *género chico* and *zarzuelas*, and dramatic actors soon began to tour in the provinces of Mexico. Although several "barrio" theatres existed in Mexico City in which varying genres were produced, only six major theatres existed in Mexico.[2] Mexican dramatic companies were booked by theatre managers in Mexico City only infrequently. Moreover, when foreign touring companies with featured "stars" arrived in Mexico City, the theatre managers quickly hired them and evicted local companies already performing in their theatres. Many Spanish and Italian opera and operetta companies appeared along with a variety of English, German, and American troupes. Motion pictures were in such demand that many theatres soon exhausted their supply and had to alternate films with "variety acts" to keep up with the demand. By the end of the 1910 season, only one theatre in the Capital was offering serious drama on a regular basis.

Dramatic companies thus displaced had toured occasionally before 1900. Better rail connections from Mexico to Texas made it possible for a larger number of Mexicans to settle in Texas than in other states. There were several Texas ports available for emigrants leaving Mexico before World War I, including Laredo, El Paso, Matamoros, and Eagle Pass. On the other hand, Arizona had only one inland port city.[3]

As the Mexico City market for serious drama declined, dramatic companies boarded trains and struck out for Texas. Some provided a quality of theatre never before seen in Texas, including such outstanding performers as Evangelina Adams, Enrique del Castillo, Prudencia Griffel, Elisa de la Maza, Francisco E. Solórzano, and Enrique Labrada.

About twenty-five dramatic acting companies are known to have performed in Texas, but it is likely there were more. The information gathered on these companies has primarily been extracted from extant Spanish-language newspapers available from this period and has been corroborated by eyewitness accounts and available private collections. There are only scant sources to indicate that at least a few of these companies appeared in other parts of the United States than those discussed here. While they occasionally appeared elsewhere, we know they appeared regularly in Texas. The available evidence indicates that there were three types: touring repertory companies, resident companies, and large combinations from Mexico City.[4] (See Appendix III for a list of the companies appearing between 1900 and 1935.)

Touring Stock Companies

Between 1900 and 1910 the touring stock company was the most common type of company. Such troupes spent most of their time in Mexico and only occasionally visited Texas. Although there are many such companies, the Compañía Sr. José Martínez de la Lastra can serve as an example since we know so much more about this company than the others.

The Compañía Dramática del Sr. José Martínez de la Lastra first appeared in Texas in 1906. We know that this company included at least 10 actors, including: Sr. José Martínez de la Lastra, Sra. Margarita Fernández, leading actor and actress; Sr. Ernesto Martínez Siliceo and his wife, Sra. Julia Siliceo, playing second-line parts; Srta. Armendina Martínez, probably the daughter of Sr. Martínez de la Lastra, playing the ingenue; and Julia and Manuel López, brother and sister, playing the leading actor and actress in comic roles, that is, the young girl (*dama joven*) and the young man (*galán joven*), respectively. At least two married couples were among the members and the Martínez de la Lastra's provided children for juvenile roles. The Martínez de la Lastra family was the nucleus of the troupe.

Based upon accounts from both the Mexican stage and from informants we can deduce that the size of companies ranged from at least 10 to no more than 30. Besides the actors and actresses, however, each company generally travelled with others. These included the: head prompter (*primer apunte*), who sat in the prompter's box; call boy (*transpunte*), who notified the actors of their entrances and exits; tailor (*sastre*), costumer (*guardaropa*), hairdresser (*peluquero*), scenic painter (*pintor escenógrafo*), someone to run the scenic machines (*maquinista*), and often a representative (*representante*) and musical director-arranger for the comic afterpieces (*maestro director y concertador*). Actors were also known to double in these service jobs.[5]

Each member of the company was responsible for a variety of duties. The company manager generally served as the director of the company as well as the leading actor. Elisa de la Maza seems to have been unique as a female director and manager, although she apparently delegated matters of touring arrangements to a representative. Except for de la Maza, the directors and managers were men. Even though actor-managers controlled the companies, the leading actress sometimes gave her name to a troupe, as for example the Compañía Evangelina Adams. This was, nevertheless, the exception rather than the rule.

The actor-managers had the final say in all matters of production. The accounts of 13 June and 20 June 1908 indicate that Martínez de la Lastra was in charge of rehearsals. The actor managers chose the scripts, were in charge of casting, ran the rehearsals and imposed necessary fines for infringement of rules of conduct, and hired musicians, painters, designers, and other personnel. They also organized the group, were ordinarily the most experienced and well-known actors of the groups, and delegated responsibilities to other members of the troupe.[6]

Typically, the actors in Mexican acting companies were shareholders in the company. The responsibilities of shareholders varied. Among them were the ownership and maintenance of costumes, advertising of performances by distribution of leaflets and broadsides prior to performances, and copying of plays. Each actor or actress was usually assigned a line of business, that is, a limited range of parts.

We have only a few indications of lines typically found in dramatic companies of the time. Typical lines of business of a Mexican dramatic company were: leading actors and directors (*primeros actores y directores*), about 4 individuals; leading comic actor (*primero en el género cómico*), 1; leading actresses (*primeras actrices*), 2; leading ingenues (*primeras damas jovenes*), 2; second-line ingenues (*segundas damas jovenes*), 2 or 3; character actors (*actores característicos*), 2; and actors (*actores*), 6. Also included were the second-line male (*segundo hombre*) and the young gallant (*galán joven*).[7]

It was the task of the director to cast actors in the specific lines required for each company. Francisco E. Solórzano was often reported in the press to be in Mexico recruiting company members. His task, however, was generally nothing more than organizing a group since most actors already had lines of business when employed. Certainly we may easily identify the director as leading actor and often the part of the leading actress was clearly established, leaving second-line parts to others. Once an actor was given a particular role, it remained his until he left the company.

An actor might have many roles assigned to him, any one of which he could be expected to perform on relatively short notice.

We know that since there was a high turnover in a company's membership, the second-line actors often were moved up in rank to succeed former members. The exception to this was when a new well-known figure joined the company in which case he or she was automatically given leading roles. Rarely did comic actors play serious roles and then only supporting ones. Although benefit performances allowed the recipient to choose the play and which members he or she preferred for the performance, the actual casting seems to have been done by the director. Of course, the benefit performance was reserved for the leading actress and, less often, the leading actor.

Plays were rehearsed by the director of the company. The account of 25 November 1905 reports that the "performance of the plays was magnificent and well directed." As to the process of preparation, the extant promptbooks of both prompters and directors indicate little more than line cuts and entrances and exits. Directors must have assumed that the actors knew their jobs and must have spent rehearsal time establishing entrances and exits. The greatest attention in the scripts is given to the opening and closing or raising and lowering of curtains. There is also an indication that crowd or group scenes were also given rehearsal time for bits of stage business, and that required group responses at crucial points in the plays, such as laughter or shouting, were well rehearsed. Specific blocking was probably minimal since the main characters generally assumed the best stage positions at center and others moved around them. The actors delivered their main dialogue directly to the audience.[8]

The actors were given "sides," that is, a copy of each actor's part with cues. Only the director and prompter held an entire script copy. The actors learned their assigned lines; only at rehearsal did they hear the entire script. The company had only one or two copies of each play. In the promptbook were made all the necessary notes relating to performance: cues for sound, music, special effects, exits and entrances, and, infrequently, lists or notations about properties.

The manager of the company generally organized the tours, although often another popular male actor would be sent ahead of the company after the end of its engagement at one theatre to arrange further appearances at the next. This may be the reason that so many of the more popular actors often left the original company to begin their own company once their popularity was well established. Since the popular male actor knew the methods of organization and operation required to make a company successful and how to organize its tours, he was well equipped to branch out on his own and doing so would certainly be more profitable for him.

Touring for many companies from Mexico became common practice. Having toured the provinces of Mexico often, coming into Texas merely extended, rather than altered, their regimen. Although there are hints of the existence of a Texas-to-California circuit as evidenced by stamps on the extant promptbooks, no further evidence of this practice has been found. Surviving members of dramatic companies recall that contractual agreements were reached between the advance man, generally the manager or his appointee, and the theatre managers. This agreement was more commonly oral than written, but company members cannot recall a breach of contract.

The established route most commonly used by companies arriving from Mexico began in Laredo. While at this time most companies did not go further, some did go to San Antonio and at least in one known instance, one went on to San Diego, Texas, en route to Matamoros, Mexico. If companies appeared in El Paso, they went through Chihuahua and Juárez rather than through Laredo. Laredo, San Antonio, and El Paso were all on the railroad route and that method of travel seems to have been the one most commonly used by the companies. Yet, most companies appeared only in Laredo and then returned to Mexico.

Performance spaces continued to be very similar to those already discussed although some spaces were more often used than others. In Laredo the Teatro Solórzano was leased by Sr. Francisco E.

Solórzano and although he was not permanently in residence there, he continually contracted with organized companies of varying genres to perform there. This theatre was an indoor hall, similar to the church halls described in the first chapter. But in addition this theatre had an outdoor patio attached to it which was also used for performances. All we can gather about the patio is that a raised platform was used when companies performed out of doors, generally during the hot summer months. There were no permanent seats in this facility nor was it designed specifically as a theatre. It was, however, at this time used only infrequently for meetings, public celebrations, or other affairs. When acting companies were not performing there, films and variety acts generally were offered.

The raised platform was the only feature distinguishing the Teatro Solórzano as a place for theatrical performances. In this theatre, however, the auditorium was divided to create categories of seating. Thus, this theatre seems to have been similar to the Teatro Salón San Fernando of San Antonio which also served as a theatrical facility for acting companies. For at least one engagement of the Compañía Solórzano the Teatro Unión was used in San Antonio, although nothing is known about that theatre's locale or facilities.

It was rare for two companies to appear simultaneously in any city but such situations did occur, as in the case when the Compañía del Castillo had to move due to the arrival of the Compañía Labrada. Most made advanced agreements, selling season tickets which guaranteed an audience and a theatre in which to seat them by the time the curtain rose. This practice was obviously necessary since few performance spaces were available in any one town.

Besides the season tickets sold, single event tickets were available as is indicated in the advertisement of 17 March 1906 which states that prices for tickets are as usual. The contractual agreements between companies and theatre managers usually were for eight performances.[9]

The Compañía Alfonso Calvó sold "economy cards" for $3.00 gold, good for eight tickets, all for one performance or spread over several. These cards were available until one week prior to the first performance. This guaranteed the company at least a minimal income prior to appearing. In some cases companies would have preferred to continue their engagements for longer periods, but the arrangements made beforehand did not allow for this.

Companies might perform on any day of the week and only unusual circumstances would cause cancellations. Since the actors played more or less the same type of characters in all plays they could perform many parts on short notice. There was a large repertory of plays in the touring company. Companies not only prided themselves in but also listed as their major feature the fact that they presented plays never before seen on Texas stages. These were advertised as new and modern or, if drawn from a traditionally well-known repertory, having been mounted with new and sumptuous decorations in which the leading actor or actress had excelled in Mexico.[10]

The bill changed daily, thus the same audience attended again and again. In fact, no touring company was known to stage consecutive performances of the same play. Such a system met the needs of actor, troupe, repertory, and audience. The troupe needed a sizeable repertory. Once plays were produced by the companies, they were retained as long as they drew audiences and evidence in promptbooks shows that many of these were revised, probably as a result of a declining popularity. There is some evidence that original native dramas were produced although none of these are known to survive. The demand for new works likely accounts for the need for original works, and original plays always had an appeal with the public. Liaisons with well-known writers that ventured into playwriting, either in Mexico or the United States, were not untypical for some companies that made lengthier stays in some cities.

Besides the agreements for engagements of eight or nine performances, companies were known to make extended engagements. The Compañía Martínez de la Lastra ended one engagement on 4 July 1908 and began another in the same place on 18 July, leaving on 22 August. Upon its departure, the Teatro Solórzano, where it had been performing, was left empty. Apparently no other company had been booked by Solórzano and the void prompted an immediate advertisement in the newspaper with an appeal to any interested company to make use of the facility. The ad specified that a company of *zarzuelas* was preferred, probably because such a company could more readily fill the vacancy by allowing Solórzano the extensive time he usually required to journey to Mexico where he often returned to carefully select, prepare and perfect new dramatic companies as he introduced them across the Mexican border.

Most troupes sought to acquire a permanent home elsewhere if they were not able to do so in Mexico City. However, forced closures of theatres due to plagues, financial difficulties, or being forced out by more popular troupes meant unusually long periods of touring. Touring entailed many problems that companies had to contend with for there were few permanent theatres outside of Mexico City. As they sought suitable places in which to perform, many unexpected circumstances occurred.

While touring, the Compañía Martínez de la Lastra experienced two difficulties which affected its performances. One of the company members died while the troupe was on tour through Lampazos, Mexico, cutting short its engagement. The other difficulty involved a matter which may have been experienced by other companies as well. While on tour in Mexico, the company was invited to inaugurate a new theatre in Sabinas Hidalgo. A local priest had been threatening the public, "in the pulpit and everywhere else," with excommunication if they attended the theatre. The newspaper account in Laredo which announced the incident quickly came to the defense of the actor-manager, pointing out that Sr. Martínez de la Lastra had the constitution of Mexico on his side because his was "an honest profession, the laws support him, because he has a business established and he pays his taxes." The account went on, "the priest is also attempting to prejudice the public against the theatres, but he cannot do that to someone who obeys the laws and is protected by them."

This event reveals much about the attitude toward Mexican theatre prior to 1910. The theatre was held in high-esteem. This incident also indicates that the government was its protector and the companies paid for that protection. Certain taxes had to be paid by companies in Mexico.

While similar fees were not required in Texas, the companies did incur several expenses. No border fees were imposed on the companies at this time. The actors themselves were responsible for their own lodging. The companies, however, covered the cost of travel, properties, and required scenery. The Compañía Martínez de la Lastra announced "spectacular and sumptuous" performances with many transformations, mutations, and apparatus along with extravagant costumes. The account of 21 April 1906 is only one of many that attest that the company performed with all of the necessary production requirements of the play.[11]

Other company expenses included the printing of programs, broadsides, tickets, and cards advertising the company's name and address to have on hand for potential business arrangements. The salary of the company members was most commonly a share of the proceeds after all operating expenses had been deducted. There is no indication of specified salaries or of guaranteed "benefit" performances being given to the company members. Occasionally, unusual circumstances such as family financial difficulties were given as a reason for some company member other than leading actors to receive a benefit performance.

Benefit performances were generally dedicated to certain individuals in the city, but these were most often the newspaper people, certain social or civic groups, or the entire city. In one case, a young actress dedicated her benefit performance "to the social circles and to the youth of Laredo," with whom she obviously had an appeal. In addition to ticket sales, benefits often prompted many gifts to the person being honored. Material rather than monetary gifts were the most common way for townspeople to show their gratitude.

Gala benefits and many evenings of performances provided Texas audiences with a unique opportunity to increase their social and cultural activities for many years. While many touring troupes performed in Texas, many that had frequented the State since the beginning of the century ceased to appear as the first decade came to a close. Such was the case with the Compañía Martínez de la Lastra. We can only gather scant information about the Compañía Martínez de la Lastra after 1908. In an account of 26 September 1908, Sr. Martínez de la Lastra had inaugurated a *"Salón de Patinar,"* a skating rink which was leased to him by the Society of Concordia which ran the Teatro Concordia. This salon was in Nuevo Laredo and Sr. Martínez de la Lastra was said to have rented the salon for a period of five months during which time it was used as both a skating rink and as a theatre, a practice which became common after 1910. The total rent taken by the Society was $1,500.00, but we do not know the amount paid by Sr. Martínez de la Lastra nor the proceeds he made while in residence there.[12]

According to the few extant accounts of Laredo, the company appeared only infrequently on Mexican American stages after 1910. In 1920 Martínez de la Lastra wrote to several former actors and company managers, suggesting they join him in forming a new company to tour as they had done so often in the past. One letter mentions the activities of former company members who had continued theatrical activities on both sides of the border. Martínez de la Lastra probably continued to work as others he mentions, either forming a resident company or continuing to tour in Mexico.[13]

While no investigation of the touring companies may answer all questions about their organization and operations, certainly some of their contributions are revealed. The companies sustained the public's interest in full-length dramas primarily of a serious nature which along with comic afterpieces made an evening both full and diverse. They also maintained an audience for theatre, produced plays never before seen in Texas, and produced original native dramas.[14] Above all, these dramatic companies were able to establish a reconnection between Mexican Americans and Mexico. Rather than isolating themselves in the United States, the Spanish-speaking communities were able to continue cultural relations with Mexico. Evidence also shows that the audiences included Anglo Americans and Italian Americans as well.

The companies continued many of the same practices they had used before 1900, but the companies were much more numerous between 1900 and 1910. Their aim of providing wholesome entertainment continued, as is evidenced by several accounts. For example, newspapers reported that the Teatro Solórzano in Laredo, "continues to offer cultural and interesting spectacles," and "the families can be assured of morality in all the performances." As further assurance to the families, the management had already "taken measures of providing security police to insure perfect order" in the galleries of the theatre. The Compañía Martínez de la Lastra guaranteed performances of "moral plays and especially works for the benefit of the families of the city." By 23 May 1908, the Teatro Solórzano announced that while it could no longer "offer notable actors and actresses," it was still able to provide "works that are clean of heart and for the entire family to enjoy, suitable for any home without a single distasteful phrase, nor inappropriate sentiment, or distasteful joke."[15]

Theatrical conditions on the Spanish-language stage differed little from those of the provincial Anglo American theatre in America. The period in which a considerable number of touring Spanish-language companies appeared was much later than for the English-language stage. Nevertheless, the basic problems and circumstances were to a large extent similar. The difficulties of the frontier and the rigors of establishing theatrical centers and an established audience were keenly felt by both groups. Companies of the highest quality along with those that could not find steady employment in the urban centers came to try their luck in the communities that were just being settled. Theatre centers had to be established, along with a theatre going public and quality performances, but audiences were willing to support companies of lesser quality.

On the English-language stage, New York set the standard and established criteria from which other theatrical ventures could be measured. The theatre in the United States patterned itself with the mother country, England, at its inception, something which Mexican theatre had done with Spain. In the beginning, visits from major actors to the provinces served to elevate the quality of provincial troupes, but as starring engagements came to be a mark of excellence, lesser actors began to tour. Eventually more and more smaller companies began appearing and the quality of performances suffered. Audiences began to grow tired of their repertory so the companies had to broaden it with variety, *entr'acte* entertainment, melodrama, and minor forms.

The broad expanse toward the American west via the railroad enabled touring companies to establish themselves outside of New York and allowed them a wide range of theatrical performances. While styles changed in New York and other metropolitan centers, theatrical forms in the provinces survived much longer. Similar circumstances are found in the patterns of Spanish-language theatrical touring in the U.S. However, the English-language provincial theatre reached its peak of activity in the first decade of the twentieth century. It offered its audiences a wide variety of entertainment and forms besides serious drama and supported a diverse theatrical establishment drawn from the popular theatre, early variety entertainments, tent shows, magicians and medicine shows. Circumstances in the Spanish-language theatre were uniquely different, for, not only was it just being established, but serious full-length drama largely dominated the performances. More importantly, while the basic producing organization initially was the resident stock company on the Anglo American stage, the Spanish-language stage in Texas was dominated by the touring company with no trace of resident companies in the first part of the century, and the repertory system prevailed.

By the end of the first decade of the twentieth century Spanish-language dramatic companies were undergoing a crisis. All was not well with the companies touring from Mexico, as is evidenced by the newspaper account of 25 July 1908 in which the Compañía "La Nacional" of Gutiérrez was said to have disbanded in Torreon, Mexico, for it had fallen a "victim of the crisis that is striking all towns in Mexico." The account made use of the term "aguela," a term associated with the economic crisis that prevailed in Mexico, worsening as time went by.[16]

Other touring companies were also affected by the changing economic conditions in Mexico, but the chaotic political, social, and cultural climate would soon not only alter the theatre significantly, but plunge the entire country into disrepair. The Compañía Calvó disbanded in Mexico due to "bad winds that run through Mexico for the dramatic art," said the account of 1 August 1908: "With this company, it now makes four in all which within the month of July disbanded--all very old, well organized, and of much prestige." The celebration of the "Great Centennial" in Mexico in 1910 commemorating the birth of Independence was intended to celebrate the "Golden Age" of Porfirio Díaz, but in fact the end of the first decade of the twentieth century served as a significant date to commemorate its demise.[17]

The Mexican Revolution began in 1910 and by 1913 had developed into full-scale civil war. The call for reform in Mexico was great and diverse. The revolt affected a broad spectrum of society, for the change was economic, nationalistic, religious, social, and political. Political reform did little to improve the conditions of the poorer classes as a series of leaders sought to rectify the dictatorial government of the Díaz regime. The conflict began in northern Mexico, along the Texas border, thus causing several companies in that area to emigrate to Texas. The revolution reached central Mexico by 1917, greatly affecting activities in that region. Turmoil in society and the economy in Mexico led to continuous strife; and this induced many more Mexican dramatic companies to cross the border to the United States, enabling the tradition of Spanish-language dramatic entertainment to continue on the American stage as a new type of Spanish-language dramatic company was formed, the resident company.

Resident Stock Companies

Itinerant stock companies still out-numbered all other types, but a new and historically significant type of company appeared between 1910 and 1915--the resident stock company. The resident companies were few and rather short-lived but played a very important role. The first of such types was that of Sr. Francisco E. Solórzano in Laredo. We may recall that Sr. Solórzano had established the Teatro Solórzano in Laredo sometime after 1900. Apparently at that time he managed the theatre that bore his name but did not own it. While he continuously booked and often organized and performed with itinerant companies of varying types, he did not permanently settle in Laredo until 1910. Initially the company he organized performed variety and short comic pieces. In an account of 23 February 1911, however, the Compañía Solórzano was said to have begun performing full-length drama. According to an advertisement for that theatre the Valdez Brothers and their company were managing and performing at the Teatro Solórzano in July of 1910, offering much diversity in entertainment. By 14 September 1911, however, the theatre was reported to be the property of Sr. Solórzano and under his sole management. Once Solórzano settled permanently in Laredo, dramatic performances by professional actors were consistently assured on a regular basis.[18]

Most of the touring companies that came to Texas between 1900 and 1910 had performed in the Teatro Solórzano for at least a short engagement. The Teatro Solórzano became an established stopping point for companies to appear when coming from Mexico. Although the company of Solórzano was the first, we know very little about his enterprise. There is, however, one company about which we do know much more due in part to surviving descendants and various collections.[19]

The Compañía Carlos Villalongín arrived in San Antonio on or about 8 May 1911. The company had contracted to perform at the Teatro Aurora, a salon converted into a theatre. The company expected to return to Coahuila, Mexico, where it held temporary residence, after completing its agreement.[20]

The Mexican Revolution made Carlos Villalongín, his family, and some other actors decide to remain in San Antonio. Although it is known that Villalongín leased the Teatro Aurora, that probably did not occur until after 1 October since the two extant broadsides concerning the company indicate that the theatre was under the management of Porfirio Garza in May and J.S. Noriega in October. Upon his arrival in town or shortly thereafter, Villalongín founded a partnership with Carlos Saldaña. Their venture was called "Compañía Lirico-Dramática Villalongín y Saldaña" and Saldaña had the leading role in the performances of 22 and 23. In that same production the leading actress was Margarita Fernández; Concepción Hernández, who had almost always played the leading role in the Compañía Villalongín, played the second-line role. (See broadsides in Appendix I.)

The Teatro Aurora was short-lived. The Compañía Villalongín merged with the Compañía Juan B. Padilla, and in mid-year of 1912, with the opening of the Teatro Zaragoza, the Compañía was hired by the theatre owner, Sam Lucchese, to perform at the new facility. The new dramatic company was so successful that by 5 May 1913, the theatre had to be enlarged. The company thus began a long engagement at the new theatre at which dramas shared the stage with film and variety. Although other smaller theatres did exist in the city, the Teatro Zaragoza, situated in the heart of the Mexican American community in San Antonio, was considered the center of Spanish-language dramatic entertainment.[21]

With the Compañía Juan B. Padilla, the Compañía Villalongín--thereafter called the Compañía Padilla--continued to work in San Antonio on a regular basis for approximately five years during which it was a significant element in the city's cultural life for it not only held a position of prominence but it established this theatre as an integral part of the Mexican American society. Villalongín continued to tour at least occasionally and when he did his company, comprised of family members, used the name Compañía Villalongín, as is evidenced by various accounts including one of a performance in Brownsville in which Villalongín performed the leading role along with Concepción Hernández.[22]

Resident companies, like that of the Teatro Zaragoza, typically changed personnel frequently. Based on family groups, such companies would lose one family and hire another. Thus, five, six, or even seven actors at a time would disappear from the bills, and shortly afterwards the company name might also change to reflect a new alliance with another family. At the Teatro Zaragoza, for instance, Padilla assumed the role of theatre manager and company manager and occasionally acted while Carlos Villalongín primarily continued as the leading man as successive mergers occurred in this and subsequent companies. When the Compañía Ricardo de la Vega arrived and began to work at the Teatro Zaragoza, the companies of Padilla and de la Vega merged. Padilla had the "leading role of Iago" in the *Othello* production of 10 November 1914 and de la Vega was named manager of the company and continued as the director.

The reviewer for the production of *Othello* attributed the principal role to Iago in the Teatro Zaragoza production due to the "poor translation and interpretation by the Spanish dramatists, F. Retes and Francisco Perez Echevarría, that the company chose to present." In fact, the reviewer did not fault the actors for the poor performance, for, he said, "they are given little material to work with," and, hence, provide "a kitten in place of a lion." Thus, while the play may have been inferior to some, Padilla's clearly was the principal role in the performance.[23] It is interesting to note that the villainous role of "Iago" was featured instead of "Othello." The role obviously had more of an appeal to the audience if Padilla, the leading actor, was assigned the role. This type of classical drama, however, was an exception to the dramatic fare in Spanish-language theatre and in no other instance is a work by Shakespeare mentioned.

Since both Villalongín and Padilla were generally known in the city as representatives of the theatre owner, at least until 1914, they probably shared supervisory responsibilities. Sam Lucchese then took over managerial responsibilities and by 1915 he had assumed the role of impresario, managing the resident company himself.

We may view the organization and practice of the Compañía Villalongín in San Antonio as typical of a resident company. The organization of that company shows several similarities to the touring companies. Company members were shareholders; the director, who was also the company manager and the leading actor, made arrangements for performances, cast roles and ran rehearsals. Actors were still employed in lines of business.

There are, however, several deviations from the practice of the itinerant companies. The company manager was now also the theatre manager, as in the case of Carlos Villalongín who leased the Teatro Aurora, and later, Juan B. Padilla who managed the Teatro Zaragoza. Since little touring was done, the responsibilities of the advance man evolved into that of promoting the performance of the company within the city and later negotiating contracts with touring companies that arrived in the city and played in the theatres they managed. Apparently such touring companies were welcome, probably owing to the variety of plays they brought to the city and the respite they offered the resident companies. The Compañía Solórzano was reported to be "working night after night" in Laredo and only infrequently toured. By 1914, then, the resident companies served as stock companies, made facilities available to touring companies which visited the city, and also supplied stock scenery, properties, costumes, as well as actors to those visiting companies.

The beginning of resident companies meant that each could work in a real theatre--that is, in a structure which was built specifically for that purpose--and the Teatro Zaragoza provides an excellent example. We know that it was built and designed specifically for staging theatrical events. This San Antonio theatre was located at 805 W. Commerce. Unfortunately, outside of the fact that it had 800 permanent seats and a "red grand drape," we know nothing about its dimensions save that it was probably like many other structures found in the city and elsewhere at that time. The Teatro Aurora, on the other hand, was on the second floor of a printing shop and was basically a room adapted to function as a theatre. What we do know about each are facts regarding theatre management.[24]

There exists a notation of payments by Carlos Villalongín to persons hired to perform certain functions for his company. The notation, found in a promptbook dated 1915, shows a list of wages for the following: music, $10; salon (or theatre), $5; printing (*imprenta*), $2.25; clean-up (*aseo*), $1; machinist or scene-shifter (*tramoyista*), $1; and prompter, .75. The total cost was $20.00. Although at this time Villalongín was no longer serving as manager at the Teatro Zaragoza, he had assumed management at the Teatro Salón San Fernando jointly with Sr. José F. Contreras. We can assume that these notations indicate the personnel required at either of these facilities. Apparently Villalongín was acting as business manager, responsible for paying those individuals. Some of those positions (such as the machinist and prompter), however, had previously been filled by company members. Since we know that both Villalongín and Padilla had been theatre managers for Lucchese, we can see what responsibilities now were in the hands of company directors acting as theatre managers. Both men were responsible for all areas of production, which included: renting the theatre from the owner, hiring musicians, paying for printing programs and advertisement, cleaning up, shifting scenery, and prompting. It is also evident that the individuals were employed separately and not hired as members of the company, since obviously none of these were shareholders as were the actors.[25]

We also learn something about the changing nature of company management, where now the duties include theatre maintenance, publicity, and theatre staff. More importantly, the company manager was serving as representative of the impresario and determining which company might perform in this particular theatre.

The hierarchy of the theatre staff, then, is headed by the theatre owner who hired a manager. As in the touring companies, the company director-manager was clearly experienced and knowledgeable of theatrical matters and thus proved vital to the theatre owner who was not. In the case of Sam Lucchese, his business was a family venture in boot-making and real estate. Having no experience in theatre management, Lucchese chose as theatre manager someone who had been a company manager, an obvious choice for the job. But the impresario's and the company manager's interests were not identical. The interest of the company manager was to secure a place for his troupe to produce plays, but the impresario's interest was return on his investment. Lucchese soon changed the original arrangement, for, by 1915, he had become his own impresario, solely responsible for hiring and firing staff, actors, and companies; he even began making trips to Mexico himself in order to secure top talent from that center of Spanish-language entertainment. Obviously, he had learned from his actor-managers and no longer had to rely on them to run his business.

Hence, a radical transformation of troupe organization resulted from the company's permanent residence, namely, actors became employees rather than independent artists, no longer running their own companies as they had before. By 1915 Lucchese determined what would be presented on stage. He contracted actors individually and also determined the length of each actor's employment, based on that individual's drawing power.

The resident director's role remained the same in terms of casting, running rehearsals, and organizing promotion from members. Yet when a company merged with another company or with visiting companies, the director no longer was in full charge but had to accommodate the visiting company's director and most often became the leading actor or merely another actor in the company. While this was often the case with Padilla, Carlos Villalongín more often preferred to work at the Teatro Salón San Fernando where he could manage his own company.

Since companies were almost always organized around a family nucleus, the fathers generally served as company managers. This is true in all the known instances of resident companies (that is, Solórzano's, Villalongín's, and Padilla's). There were about 15 actors with the original Compañía Villalongín, but by 1911 several children and other family members had joined the company and increased its number to at least 25, including a prompter, property master, scene carpenter, and perhaps a scene painter, although the last may have been a temporary employee rather than a company member. Out of 15 members, five were of the Hernández-Villalongín families that had formed the company core since its inception in Mexico. Other families in the troupe included at least three: the Berrones, Padillas, and Garcías. However, companies soon became much smaller, numbering from five to ten members with the core of the company drawn from the family (that is, children and relatives) of the director and leading man. Carlos Villalongín, once established in San Antonio, added his children to the company as they became able to fill appropriate roles. In order to reduce expenses, many amateurs were also used, and if paid at all were paid only a nominal sum. Doubling of roles became increasingly common. The resident company of Solórzano also shows a change in number of company members. Hence, we can gather that, principally for economic reasons, the companies became smaller.[26]

The theatre managers were now responsible for advertising the plays to be performed. Extant broadsides announcing performances of the Compañía Villalongín before 1910 show the company as responsible. Those printed for the performance that occurred at the Teatro Aurora after 1910 illustrate that the management was making the announcements, with messages from both managers, Garza and, later, Noriega. (See Appendix I.) It must be noted, however, that few such broadsides are found after 1911, probably because they were replaced by advertisements in local Spanish-language newspapers. Such advertisements were paid for by the theatre managers rather than company managers.

A major difference between company practice before and after 1910 is in the actors' lines of business. In some instances, former leading actors and actresses had to take subordinate roles when companies merged. Also while actors were still employed according to lines of business they also had to master both comic and serious roles. By 1915 the repertory of the Villalongín company included almost twice as many *zarzuelas* as dramas and *comedias*. That same list indicates that few new plays were added to the repertory--only 7 of the total 97 works performed during the season which lasted from January 28 to March 28.

Since company members outside of the family often came and went, reshuffling of roles was common as can be seen from the varying cast lists and many erasures in the promptbooks. There was also a need to alter casts since companies were smaller and thus actors were required to play a wide variety of roles.

The resident companies, in order to reduce overhead, employed only a nucleus of professional actors and filled out casts with inex-

perienced and untrained performers who required considerable tu-
toring. This situation made it difficult for the more experienced actors to perfect their roles and as a consequence more rehearsal
time was required. Thus, rules governing conduct of rehearsals became more rigorous.

We know that the resident companies that appeared at the
Teatro Aurora did rehearse since the broadsides mention the
works "being prepared." Also announced were upcoming dramas,
something that had not appeared previously. This was probably
due to the fact that companies were now making more extended or
indefinite stays whereas before they were contracted for limited
engagements made up of a few performances of plays already in
the company's repertory. An analysis of the bill gives insights into
the rehearsals.

After 1910, the bills showed a significant change. When Carlos
Villalongín first came to San Antonio to perform at the Teatro Aurora, the theatre manager expected one act of a full-length drama
to be presented each evening, along with films and variety acts,
thereby giving the public much diversity in performance. Villalongín prided himself (as do his descendants) on establishing the
practice of providing a full-length drama in a single evening, with
no interruptions and no incidental entertainment. Whether it was
Villalongín alone or he along with others, it meant that he had to
build an audience willing to accept an entire evening devoted to a
single full-length drama. The only interruptions were the usual two
intermissions between acts. By 1913, Villalongín and Padilla had
made popular the single play bill on a regular basis at the Teatro
Zaragoza.[27]

By 1913 the Compañía Villalongín performed only on weekends
and Thursdays. The company performed a single full-length play
from its repertory on each of these evenings. Prior to 1910, performances generally began at 9:30 p.m., but at the Aurora the
company was scheduled to begin at 7:30 p.m. Noticeable changes
in the type of performances were evident in the advertisements
which appeared. The drama *Chucho el roto* of May 1911 is said to
be "varied and of that select old repertory one may recall of the

past." (See broadside in Appendix I.) No longer did announcements indicate that performances were "new and never before
seen." The management promised the public that although "you
may have seen *Chucho el roto* recently performed by another company, this is the true version, I can guarantee." Plays were no
longer announced as "sensational, splendid, grand drama," probably
because resident companies did not have all the required decorations and apparatus for the full spectacle they had once been able
to provide. The economic factor cannot be overlooked, for such
productions were costly and extravagant and generally out of the
range that resident companies could now afford. As the companies
continued their permanent residence in the cities, generally serving
the same audience, the need for new plays increased.

The fact that the resident companies began looking for new
dramas contributed to the emergence of native Texas Mexican
American dramatists. While this was not unique to the resident
companies, with permanent residence the motivation increased.
Although enough evidence exists to indicate that original plays
were written, none of the scripts have been found to date. There
are also no records available to show whether the few dramatists
that resided in Texas and infrequently provided plays for performance were paid for the use of their dramas. The honor of production, however, was clearly one compensation.

Carlos Villalongín did much to create native drama by the mere
fact that he and his company remained in Texas permanently. He
developed associations with several newspaper editors who were
"aficionados" of the stage and who made attempts to write plays, often offering them to the Compañía Villalongín. Manuel Musquiz
Blanco, one of several editors of the popular and powerful newspaper, *La Prensa*, had written *Almas rusticas*, a drama that had
been produced by the company prior to 1910 and continued as one
of their regularly performed plays. Musquiz Blanco was known to
dedicate his dramas to Carlos Villalongín, and continued to write in
San Antonio during the revolutionary years of Mexico. One of the
promptbooks of three plays copied by Carlos Villalongín has a
dedication to Villalongín by Musquiz Blanco:

> To my good and dear friend, the actor Don Carlos Villalongín, in whom the Lic. Bruno [the main character] in *Almas rusticas* has come alive, true life, breathing with reality. My work it was, it then became yours--thus I dedicate this drama to you who has lived and felt it. There is nothing else to do but give you what is yours.
> M. Musquiz Blanco in Parras, 29 July 1907.[28]

We can see that the association between the two men began before both came to San Antonio. Musquiz Blanco was one among many who sought refuge in San Antonio from the political struggle that occurred in Mexico. He remained in San Antonio at least until 1923. The large touring company of María del Carmen Martínez premiered another of his plays, *Los de abajo*.[29]

One popular and well attended occasion was the benefit performance, a gala affair in the city. It generally brought a large attendance and was looked upon as a social event for primarily invited guests. Admission to the event was handled by the company manager. This did not change until after 1915 when the owner became the manager and began handling all aspects of special performances and receiving the larger share of the proceeds.

Extensive accounts of performances were always carried in the newspaper *La Prensa* in San Antonio, some of which were benefit performances "for the editors" or "for the good of the publication." It is probable that some arrangements existed between the company and the editors, since stories but no conventional advertisements appear for performances at the Teatro Zaragoza until about 1914. Often benefits were held for various projects in the Mexican American community, such as the "Function of Love" in November of 1914 sponsored by the Compañía Ricardo de la Vega when the company was working jointly with that of Padilla in November of 1914. This function was organized to "benefit the widows and orphans of the revolution," who "suffer so terribly in the internal war which drains the vitality of our beloved Mexico little by little." In 1911 the Compañía Solórzano performed a benefit for the "Congreso Mexicanista," an organization to aide and represent the Mexican American community in Laredo, an event which produced

$22.27 in contributions. The resident companies gave such benefit performances more often than touring groups did. It is understandable that members of the company had to take an active part in the social life of the city as a means of promoting their business.[30]

Although the resident stock company was rather short-lived and was eventually undermined by the extended engagements of the touring star combinations, the former contributed greatly to the success of the latter. Four such contributions may be noted. First, as theatre managers saw the need to build a thriving, successful business, they increased the promotion of that business. Second, it is also with this type of company that we see the rise of the first native Mexican American actors as well, since the children born to company members tended to remain within the State and continue in their parents' profession. Third, some evidence exists of native Mexican American drama which rose from the demand by the permanent companies for new plays, and, most significantly, fourth, since they provided dramatic entertainment on a regular basis as they firmly established an audience for such activity, the resident companies made the theatre a permanent part of the culture and the community.

On the English-language stage in America, the resident repertory companies were the basic producing organization through the 19th century. The 35 permanent companies of 1850 rose to about 50 in 1870. Yet, these companies were eventually undermined by the rise of travelling productions. While many touring companies performed in smaller, more remote areas of the country, there was an ever increasing dependence on visiting stars. The star system gradually gave way to the combination company which included a star, a complete cast, and all of the necessary production elements. The resident stock companies soon decreased. The long run greatly damaged the repertory system, and the fifty permanent companies of 1870 had diminished to eight by 1880, four by 1887, and virtually disappeared by 1900. A resurgence of this type of company did occur in the late 1880s, although this was a low-budget, popular-priced company rather than the first-class organization producing new plays that we had seen before. These lower-priced companies gradually increased and by World War I there were about 120.[31]

Perhaps the most prominent difference between the English-language and the Spanish-language stages in America was that the rise and demise of the resident stock company had occurred so much earlier on the English-language stage. The Mexican American resident companies had not even gotten underway until the end of the first decade of the twentieth century. Nevertheless, between 1910 and 1915 they thrived and thereafter tried from time to time to reorganize and find new affiliations with theatres, particularly when touring companies and other attractions were not available.

The period between 1910 and 1915 saw much growth in theatrical activity due to continuous political upheaval in Mexico. Clearly, if the Mexican revolution of 1910 had not occurred, Mexican dramatic companies probably would not have come to Texas on such a large scale and remained for such a long time, in some instances on a permanent basis. Such companies left seemingly lucrative businesses in Mexico, and many remained in Texas to found centers of theatrical activity that still remain today.

By establishing Spanish-language theatres and arranging accommodations for touring companies, the resident companies contributed to their own demise. The touring companies became increasingly more numerous after 1915 but, more importantly, by 1917 the combination companies began arriving in San Antonio, Laredo, and El Paso, where they were guaranteed both audiences and theatres in which to perform.

Combination Companies[32]

Combination companies (that is, those which travel with star and full company), were less frequently seen on the Mexican American stage than other kinds of companies, but nevertheless these had considerable impact on the practice and policies of the other types. These combination companies arrived primarily from the Mexican stage, although some Spanish companies also appeared. The

Compañía Virginia Fábregas is an excellent example of this type. Others included the Compañía Dramática Mercedes Navarro which performed in El Paso in 1919; the "Gran Compañía Dramática Mexicana" of Rosita Arriaga which performed in El Paso in 1920; and the Compañía María Guerrero from Spain, which featured the actress and her husband, Fernando Díaz de Mendoza, appeared as late as 1927 in San Antonio. While these combination companies featured female stars, others featured male stars such as the Compañía Dramática Ricardo Mutio, erstwhile leading actor with the Compañía Virginia Fábregas.

The first documented combination company arrived in Texas in 1917, although there is evidence that the star of that company may have appeared in Texas or near the border in 1899. The Compañía Virginia Fábregas, which won international stature by 1917, displayed the talent of Virginia Fábregas who had begun her career on the Mexican stage in 1892 at the age of 20. By 1917, she was recognized as the most significant dramatic actress on the Mexican stage. When she married the actor Francisco Cardona they formed a dramatic company that not only performed regularly in Mexico City, but soon began to tour in the provinces of Mexico, in Latin America, and in Spain. Finally, the star and her actor-manager husband built a theatre in Mexico City. By securing their own theatre, they avoided the situation which caused the demise or departure of most dramatic companies in the capital city, namely, having their engagements terminated by theatre owners.[33]

In Mexico, combination companies were commonly found prior to 1900, but came to Texas only infrequently until after 1915. The Compañía Virginia Fábregas may serve as representative of combination companies in Texas. This company first appeared in Texas at the end of 1917, again in 1919, 1923, 1926, and finally in 1928 to inaugurate the reconstructed Teatro Nacional of San Antonio.

Fábregas and Cardona divorced in 1911 and Cardona closed their theatre. Before long the Mexican government took possession of the theatre for taxes, renaming it "Municipal Cooperative." Fábregas formed her own company and toured extensively. In 1917, her company had just returned from an extended stay in

Madrid, Spain. Once the Compañía Fábregas returned to Mexico City, Sra. Fábregas discovered that the Teatro Fábregas was no longer available to her. Upon her return, Fábregas set out on a tour of northern Mexico in order to gather the necessary funds to regain her theatre. The company returned to Mexico City and did not set out on its next tour until December 1917. Virginia Fábregas had been contracted to make films of her two greatest successes, *El cardenal* and *La mujer x*. She thus set out on an extensive tour with her company that would terminate in Los Angeles. The company thus arrived in Texas by railroad, appearing first in Laredo, then San Antonio, and with plans to perform in El Paso. The company, however, did not appear in El Paso, for once it left Laredo it encountered immigration problems which affected attendance in San Antonio. Thus, it returned to Laredo where it had been quite successful and remained there for two weeks. Upon ending the engagement in Laredo it announced that it was returning to Mexico rather than continuing westward.

The company with which the star, Virginia Fábregas, appeared in Texas had been formed in Spain and had arrived in Mexico with five works in its repertory. By June 1917 the repertory had increased to 13 works. This number of plays is rather small in comparison to the 39 known works her company had been performing prior to her departure in 1911. Although some of her former company members were among those contracted for the tour into Texas, she also hired Luis Martínez Tovar as her leading man. Martínez Tovar had been with the company before 1911 but had returned to Spain, his homeland, where he had attained success working with the Compañía Guerrero-Mendoza, and had starred in other companies in Spain. The company that set out for Texas in December 1917 was touring with a female and male star in five plays which both stars had made famous. With this type of organization they introduced the practice of giving a number of consecutive performances of a single play featuring "stars" (a term which had not previously been used in the Spanish-language newspapers), a practice which was new to the Mexican American stage.

In Fábregas' company, there were thirty members, some of whom were Spanish in origin, a direct result of her recent tour in Spain. The accounts regarding the performances, however, ordinarily mention only a few of the actors and actresses. Attention was primarily given to Sra. Fábregas' performance and the manner in which the leading and supporting male actors assisted her.

The attention given to the leading actors clearly distinguished this type of company from the other types already discussed. The major feature of the combination company was the star. Virginia Fábregas always played the leading female role, but by frequently replacing or alternating the leading male actor she often introduced young and popular new stars to the Mexican or Spanish stage.

No known circuit ever existed in Texas. The Fábregas company had a manager who travelled in advance of the company to make the necessary arrangements. Herbert Schraeter, the manager, was neither an actor nor a director, something which distinguished him from typical practice in company management in both touring and resident stock companies. He travelled in advance of the company to make the necessary arrangements. He was not the principal spokesman for the company, however, as is evidenced in the case of an actor who was faced with problems about being admitted to Texas; in this instance, it was Fábregas who remained behind with the actor to straighten matters out.

Virginia Fábregas was in charge of a wide range of production matters. She alternated the role of director with Sr. Martínez Tovar although it is probable that she supervised and approved all elements of the production. She was always the major spokesperson for the company.

It is unclear what the role of the director was in the Fábregas combination since there was little time for rehearsal once on tour. The company made brief appearances in each town and matinee performances were often added to the already tight schedule. Thus, there was little time available for rehearsal. Nevertheless, although the Teatro Strand in Laredo continued to show films and variety acts throughout the afternoon, the other theatres used by this company were generally empty prior to performances and at least brief rehearsals could have been held at those venues. We can gather, however, that the productions were already well prepared prior to the company's arrival. Certainly the production elements were complete (that is, "the decorations, mise en scene, and luxury which make this company one of the most complete" to ever arrive in Laredo). The productions had been rehearsed, prepared, and presented first in Spain and again in Mexico City prior to the company's tour. In the account of 26 December 1917, the performance was said to have been so well-studied that the prompter had little work to do.[34]

Besides the actual cast members, backstage personnel toured with the company. These included property men, seamstresses (to maintain all costumes), and grips (to handle scenery). In the case of the company's tour of 1926, the "sumptuous decoration of the great scenographer, Salvador Tarazona of Mexico, would be presented for the first time," in each city that the company appeared in, and each play would have its own new scenery prepared with all of the "high demands [fastidiousness] typical of what Virginia Fábregas expects." This comment indicates that Sra. Fábregas herself had high standards for her productions.[35]

As to the actors themselves, we know that several introduced by Virginia Fábregas left her company and appeared again and again on the Mexican American stages of Texas. They either organized their own companies or joined others.

Much of the information that can be gathered about combination companies comes from Sr. Lalo Astol, whose mother, Socorro Astol, was a notable Mexican dramatic actress after Sra. Fábregas retired. Sr. Astol toured with his mother from his earliest years and recalls many details which can be corroborated by newspaper accounts and the recollections of others. He has extensive experience as an actor with his father's company, Compañía Azteca. His father, Sr. Leonardo F. García, was a former prompter on the Mexican stage and subsequent director-manager of his touring company in Texas. Both Sr. García and Sr. Astol eventually settled in Texas.

According to Sr. Astol, the actors in a combination company were not shareholders. We know that the common practice of Virginia Fábregas and her husband, Francisco Cardona, when they managed the Teatro Fábregas prior to 1911, was to pay each actor a salary. According to an account of 20 November 1917, each actor was contracted individually. The practice probably continued thereafter.[36]

From the repertory presented by this company, we can see that it featured such strong female roles as *La mujer x* (Madam X), *La castellana* (The Castilian Woman), and *El genio alegre* (The Happy Heart). The performances in each town were few, usually numbering three and no more than five in any one engagement, and Sra. Fábregas played a small number of roles. The repertory was primarily comprised of modern plays, consisting of those roles which Sra. Fábregas had made famous. Virginia Fábregas was usually the central figure in each performance, but at least once Martínez Tovar was, as in the performance of "El Interprete de Hamlet" or "The Interpretation of Hamlet." In this instance, Martínez Tovar had an opportunity to become the center of attention and show his talents. Fábregas, however, followed with performances of *El cardenal* and *La mujer x* within the same week, her two greatest successes on the Mexican stage. The Álvarez Quintero's *El genio alegre* was her choice for the matinee performance that same week.

There is no indication that Virginia Fábregas ever appeared in comic roles. She performed in serious dramas, sometimes melodramas, and most often plays from "the modern theatre." The initial announcement of her arrival from Spain in San Antonio stated that the company had a grand repertory of new plays:

> of the best Spanish and French authors. It [the company] consists of not only a homogenous group but also an archive in which appear the latest productions of Benavente, Linares Rivas, Parker, Bernstein, and others.[37]

These names were of dramatists of the modern theatre whose works were seen on both the Spanish and Mexican stages. Rodolfo Usigli, writing of the Mexican theatre in the twentieth century, says that "thanks to" Virginia Fábregas, the Mexican stage has been introduced:

> to the most successful works on European stages, done with the same luxuriousness, but with good taste, which was previously unknown on our stages where the sets, the backdrops, the refinement in production were, all in all, a bit less than unknown. Donnay, Capus, Hervieu, Lavedan (Brieux, Hermant), Benavente, the Álvarez Quinteros, the best of the French and Spanish repertories, have paraded through the theatres wherever Virginia Fábregas appeared. . . . Now she turns toward Eugene O'Neill and Pirandello with indefatigable enthusiasm.[38]

The troupe catered to the Mexico City theatre and took most of the plays from it. The plays of avant-garde Spanish dramatists along with the most modern European and American plays appeared in the troupe's bill on the Mexican stage and soon after on the Mexican American stage. Upon Jacinto Benavente's brief appearance in San Antonio en route from New York to Mexico, Fábregas performed in a tribute to him with one of his works, *Rosas de otoño* (Roses of Autumn). Fábregas was the first to present Pirandello in San Antonio in *All for the Best*, produced in 1926 at the Teatro Nacional. She also presented two of Oscar Wilde's plays there, *A Woman of No Importance* and *Lady Windemere's Fan*, in the same year.

There is enough evidence in the advertisements to indicate that Mexican American audiences were able to enjoy "popular dramas" selected to appeal to the broadest possible range of tastes along with avant-garde drama. While audiences were probably not comprised of a conservative or provincial segment of society since they did attend the modern plays presented, the full-houses in the theatres wherever Fábregas appeared show that, above all, people were anxious to see the performances of the Compañía Fábregas. The star, Virginia Fábregas, however, played a major role in determining the types of her company's productions.[39]

Through accounts about the performances, we can see that the nature of acting in combinations changed markedly. Not only did all the attention have to be focused on the leading actress and often her leading man, but new types of plays and extended runs of particular productions made changes in acting almost inevitable. There were several evident changes. First, there was more time for rehearsal and familiarity with the play since fewer plays were produced while on the road. Second, actors were no longer employed for their expertise in lines of business but rather because of their popularity. Third, supporting actors were expected to maintain the center of attention on the stars in their performances, omitting any business that would detract from that focus. Fourth, there was a trend toward realism on the stage both in production elements and in acting style with the introduction of plays from the modern theatre. Fifth, omitting afterpieces and presenting a single dramatic work as an evening's entertainment placed an additional responsibility on the actor to provide excellence in a single presentation, and sixth, the company had built a reputation prior to arriving in Texas and audiences were expecting that the company would live up to it.

The attention given to the star was something new in the newspaper reviews of dramatic performances. Prior to the appearance of combination companies, reviews generally mentioned adequate performances, but the commentary was primarily centered on the plot, unfolding of the story, themes, and ideas. The Compañía Fábregas was not only highly skilled, providing an excellent star and a supporting cast, but also gave the audience "an extravagant performance." Unlike many English-language combination companies of this time, the Spanish-speaking combination companies did not travel with a single production, but the number of productions was far fewer than had been typical of earlier touring companies. The repertory was usually comprised of about five productions, both new plays and those in which the stars of the company had won national and often international acclaim.[40]

What we know of the composition and organization of the Fábregas combination company enables us to determine much about the nature of its operation. We know that the three major stops on the railroad routes that swept through Texas were Laredo, San Antonio, and El Paso. The trip from Mexico City to Laredo was along a direct route at this time, one which continued on to San Antonio. In San Antonio an east to west route made El Paso easily accessible. The Compañía travelled by train, moving from one to another of these stops within one day's time. Sr. Astol, who travelled from Mexico City to Laredo several times between 1915 and 1925 recalls that the trip took an entire twenty-four hours. He adds, however, that companies were often hampered by the fighting along the way during these years of civil war. After a time, companies became used to unexpected delays and to seeing the terrible results of the fighting. After its initial tour, the Compañía Fábregas usually performed in the cities of Laredo, San Antonio, and El Paso. In 1919 its tour extended from Mexico to Los Angeles. An account of 27 February indicates the schedule: "After a brilliant tour through California and currently now in El Paso, the company will go to San Antonio and then to Laredo on its way to Mexico." According to another account, this plan was altered somewhat: "Now it seems sure that the company will not appear in Laredo on their way back to Mexico," choosing instead to return through Eagle Pass since that border entry into Mexico now included several cities, such as Piedras Negras and Torreon, which were not only well-populated but becoming rather active in theatrical entertainment.[41]

Besides their rather brief appearances, the combination companies were unique in another respect. These companies performed in theatres which were generally not available to Spanish-language acting companies. Such facilities were larger than those commonly used by the Mexican American touring or resident companies. In Laredo the Compañía Virginia Fábregas performed at the Royal Opera House and later at the Teatro Strand; in El Paso it performed at the Texas Grand Theatre; and in San Antonio it appeared at Beethoven Hall. These theatres were also not situated in the Mexican American communities and were typically frequented by non-Spanish speakers. The seating arrangements indicate that the audiences that attended the Fábregas performances represented a broad spectrum of society. For the performance of 12 December 1917, as an example, the prices at the Royal Opera House of Laredo indicate four different seating areas: (1) the orchestra (*platea*), $1.25; (2) the first two or three rows of cushioned seats directly behind the orchestra (*luneta*), $1.00; (3) the limited seating in the gallery, .50; and (4) the general gallery, .25. Subseason tickets (*abonos*) were also available at $3.00 for the first three rows and for $2.50 elsewhere. These subseason tickets admitted the bearer to each performance given by the company, excluding extra performances which might be added afterward. Added performances were generally benefits for the leading actress or both leading actress and actor. The subseason tickets were sold prior to the arrival of the company in the city. The Compañía Fábregas refused to appear until all of these tickets had been sold, thus guaranteeing that all expenses to the company would be covered.

According to all available accounts the Compañía Fábregas was so popular that it never had any difficulty in selling these tickets almost immediately after they went on sale. The Compañía generally used the box offices of the theatres in which it was performing or as in the case of the San Antonio theatres, often the St. Anthony Hotel sold tickets. Tickets for its performances were rarely sold within the Mexican American community. There is only one instance--for its engagement in Laredo of 24, 25, and 26 December 1917--when the popular local Mexican bakery "El Gallo" was used as a ticket outlet. In fact, for the five performances in Laredo of December 1917, scalpers were able to resell tickets at double the original price.

The Compañía Fábregas always performed on two or three consecutive days, and these could be any days of the week. The bill was generally as follows: (1) an orchestral overture (the musicians were probably supplied by the management, a regular practice at this time) and (2) a full-length drama. The benefit performance given at the Teatro Strand in Laredo indicates one of the few exceptions: (1) symphony by the orchestra, (2) the two-act drama, *La garra*, and (3) the one-act *comedia*, *La cuerda floja*. This is the only known instance in which this company included an afterpiece in its bill. It is unknown whether this piece was comic or serious since the term *comedia* may refer to either form. It was offered for the occasion of the benefit performance of Sra. Fábregas, but there is no indication that she performed in the *comedia* and she probably did not. It was probably an afterpiece and the company probably travelled with skilled performers in comic lines to perform in these exclusively. This program began at 2 p.m., but most other performances began at 8:30 with the doors opening at 8 p.m. The differences between the bill of this period and those of previous eras are several. First, the drama was now the focus of the evening; second, the audiences were there to see unfamiliar serious modern drama ranging from three to six acts and lasting at least three hours; and third, the audiences came to see well established stars rather than comic short pieces or other variety entertainment.

We know that border fees were among the expenses incurred by the company. Informants indicate that it was common to pay such fees at this time, but the fees were minimal. Advertisement was a regular expense. The Compañía Fábregas used large paid ads which appeared in Spanish-language newspapers at least two days prior to the first performance and thereafter on the days of performance; no advertisements for any Mexican American events appeared in English-language newspapers. It is unknown whether handbills were distributed, but informants indicate that by this time word of mouth and billboards outside the theatres were the major sources of information regarding coming events. Nonpaid articles in Spanish-language newspapers were another major source of information.

Whatever the expenses of the company, they certainly did not keep it from realizing a substantial profit. The tour of the Mexican states just prior to her arrival in Texas had brought Sra. Fábregas "enough to be able to return to her theatre in Mexico City and rebuild it"--370,000 pesos. Whatever arrangements were required for the usually successful touring of this company, they apparently were organized well, as attested by the general success of the company and the satisfaction of its audiences.[42]

As smoothly as things may have generally gone, difficulties occasionally occurred. In 1917, the Compañía Fábregas performed in Laredo without problems and with success and had already made arrangements for performances in San Antonio and thereafter in El Paso. With subseason tickets already sold, and advertisements printed in the local newspapers, the company could not meet its agreements. One of the company members encountered immigration problems in Laredo and could not go to San Antonio as scheduled. It required word from Washington to straighten matters out, but money had by that time been returned for a sold out engagement, and a rescheduled performance drew fewer patrons than expected.

Immigration problems occurred in part due to the first World War. The war caused a mass repatriation of Mexican Americans to Mexico, especially since Mexico was experiencing a more stable political and economic climate and improved conditions seemed evident. Unfortunately, the Mexican constitution offered a sense of hope but resulted in short-lived promises. Immigration problems became increasingly more evident and border crossing more difficult; we cannot overlook the fact that the United States also wished to retain its primary labor force within the country. By 1930 it was no longer a matter of course for Mexican companies to cross the border. The arrangements for doing so included for each person: (1) a fee of $1.00 or more, (2) a visa, (3) a letter from the contracting manager on the U.S. side of the border, and (4) proof of citizenship and legal residence. Difficulties eventually became insurmountable for the travelling troupes. The appearance of such companies became more and more infrequent. By 1935 the demise of the Spanish-language dramatic companies was evident. Their history on the American stage was long-lived and they made their own unique contribution to the annals of theatre history.

The arrival of Spanish-language combination companies influenced the practice and performance of the touring stock companies. The newer companies not only introduced new plays, but the public compared the performances of well-known actors and actresses to the older companies that toured year after year, and they preferred the "stars." Also, touring stock companies could not offer productions as elaborate as those of the combinations because of the cost of scenery, costumes, and properties.

Both combination and the large touring companies included actors and actresses who remained in Texas to found worthwhile ventures by organizing their own companies or joining others already touring the State. An excellent example of this is María del Carmen Martínez who first performed in Texas in 1915. She returned in 1917 with her company, and after being exiled from Mexico, took refuge in Texas and toured further and further afield through the years. Her leading actor, Manuel Cotera, formed a company in 1921 which included many members of the Villalongín family. Although Cotera eventually returned to Mexico, the Compañía Azteca, directed by Sr. Lalo Astol's father, Sr. Leonardo F. García, evolved out of the Compañía Cotera. In 1935 García was taking the company on an extensive tour scheduled to terminate in California where he expected to remain indefinitely. But García died unexpectedly and the company disbanded, although some of its members did go on to Los Angeles where they continued to be active on the stage.

As combination companies displaced the touring stock and resident companies, theatres became larger to meet the demands of a growing public and the touring stock companies were forced to perform in the smaller Texas Spanish-speaking communities. Gradually the touring companies began to include cities not previously visited but which were becoming accessible by train, automobile or truck. In 1918, the Compañía María del Carmen Martínez appeared at the Teatro Washington in Brownsville and in 1919 the company of Manuel Cotera began one of its many tours through southwest Texas. In 1926 the Compañía Azteca made a very successful tour through Hebbronville, Benavides and San Diego which began in June and by August had travelled through Mercedes, Pharr, and Mission, Texas.

The small valley towns which had not been on the touring routes earlier became regular stops for many companies. Rio Grande City and all the small valley towns between that city and Brownsville were part of the new theatrical circuit for Spanish-language troupes. By 1928 even the Compañía Fábregas included the cities of McAllen and Rio Grande City in their tour, and in 1930 the Compañía María del Carmen Martínez performed at the Teatro Chapultepec in East Donna near Edinburg. But probably the greatest contribution of the combination companies was that they broadened the audiences of Spanish-language entertainment as they appeared in theatres outside of the immediate Mexican American community.

We can briefly turn our attention to the English-language stage to comprehend similarities and differences between the two stages. By 1895 the travelling road show had become the usual source of theatrical entertainment on the English-language stage. New York was the major theatrical center and the primary goal was the long-run hit. The problems of booking, defaults in agreements, and greed were some of the many reasons that led to the formation of "The Syndicate." A small group of men managed to gain control of the Anglo American theatre due to the complex process of negotiations between the many producers and local managers of theatres. The Anglo American theatre for the most part soon became a commercial venture. The combination system was at its height between 1900 and 1910, entertaining a large nation-wide audience. But soon the public was demanding more stars as road managers were sending out second-rate actors and shabby productions misrepresented as original New York companies. Movies, on the other hand, could offer famous stars and polished productions at more reduced prices. Soon fewer theatres were available for legitimate drama as more and more theatres turned to the movies, and the number of productions going on tour was also decreasing.[43]

The Spanish-language theatre in Texas did not suffer at the hands of a theatrical monopoly similar to the Syndicate. There were no established circuits, which made matters rather difficult for companies wishing to tour in the United States. Yet, combination companies were able to reach new territories not only due to the theatrical centers established by resident companies, but also because of their own acclaim and drawing power in communities both inside and outside of Spanish-speaking theatrical centers. These companies never offered only a single production as they toured, and their appearances were always brief. Yet, the audiences awaited them eagerly for they represented the best performers and quality performances from the Mexican theatre that audiences often read about in the U.S. Founded on the repertory system, the combination companies largely continued the practice of offering more than one production on their tours, but these productions were limited to a select few that stood out as exceptional and often the latest attractions that they had to offer.

Since it was the performance which drew the audiences to the theatres and the desire to see their favorite personalities in popular and modern dramas, we must turn to the actual performance, investigate the presentation of these plays and the contributions of the performers and the other production elements to their appeal.

Notes

1. Oscar G. Brockett, *History of the Theatre*, 5th ed. (New York: Allyn and Bacon, Inc., 1987) 476-479, 518-532, 581-589.

2. Luis Reyes de la Maza, *El teatro en México* (Mexico: U.N.A.M., 1953-1970) 1900-1910: 23, 47, 49, 60. The 6 major theatres listed are: Teatro Principal, Teatro Renacimiento (renamed Teatro Fábregas in 1911), Teatro Colón, Teatro Hidalgo, Teatro Lírico, and Teatro Arbeu.

3. Leon C. Metz, *City at the Pass: An Illustrated History of El Paso* (California: Windsor Publications, Inc., 1980) 40-41. Ricardo Romo, "The Urbanization of Southwestern Chicanos in the Early Twentieth Century," *New Scholar* 6 (1977): 194.

4. Sra. María Luisa Villalongín de Santos, former company member and daughter of the actor-manager, Carlos Villalongín, owns her father's memoirs as well as several plays, broadsides, photos, and memorabilia collected from her father and her relatives' belongings. Sr. Lalo Astol's memoirs and a large collection of his father's (Leonardo F. García) promptbooks and repertory have recently been acquired by the Mexican American Library Collection of the Latin American Library at The University of Texas at Austin. Sr. Astol's daughter, Sra. Otila Garza, also owns a private collection of materials that provide information about various companies. Among the extant collections, the most vast is the Hernández-Villalongín Collection at The University of Texas at Austin. Interviews with Sra. Maria Luisa Villalongín de Santos and Sr. Lalo Astol, San Antonio, May 1981; Sra. Otila Garza, Austin, May 1981.

5. *El Demócrata Fronterizo*, Laredo 10 March 1906: 4; 22 April 1905: 3; 21 September 1907: 2; 5 November 1904: 1.

6. *El Demócrata Fronterizo* 13 June 1908: 1; 20 June 1908: 2.

7. Manuel Mañon, *Historia del Teatro Principal de México* (Editorial Cultura, Mexico, 1932) 112, 143.

8. *El Demócrata Fronterizo* 25 November 1905: 2.

9. *El Demócrata Fronterizo* 17 March 1906:2.

10. *El Demócrata Fronterizo* 22 April 1905: 3; 21 September 1907: 2.

11. *El Demócrata Fronterizo* 17 March 1906: 2; 21 April 1906: 3.

12. *El Demócrata Fronterizo* 26 September 1908: 4; 12 December 1908: 2; *Evolución*, Laredo 23 December 1917.

13. Letter in the private collection of Sra. María Luisa Villalongín de Santos, San Antonio, Texas.

14. *El Demócrata Fronterizo* 3 March 1906: l; 20 June 1908: 4; 8 August 1908:2.

15. *El Demócrata Fronterizo* 23 May 1908: 2; 14 April 1906:2; 23 May 1908: 2.

16. *El Demócrata Fronterizo* 25 July 1908:2.

17. *El Demócrata Fronterizo* 1 August 1908:1.

18. *La Crónica*, Laredo 16 July 1910: 3; 23 February 1911: l; 22 October 1911: 4; 14 September 1911: l. See Elizabeth C. Ramírez, "Compañía Teatro Solórzano," in Weldon B. Durham, ed., *American Theatre Companies, 1888-1930* (New York: Greenwood Press, 1987) 413-416.

19. See Elizabeth C. Ramírez, "Compañía Villalongín," in Durham 449-453.

20. "Memoirs of Carlos Villalongín," in the private collection of Sra. Villalongín de Santos, San Antonio, Texas. Interview with Sra. Villalongín de Santos, San Antonio, May 1981.

21. See Elizabeth C. Ramírez, "Compañía Juan B. Padilla," in Durham 353-358.

22. "Memoirs of Carlos Villalongín," 92-93.

23. *La Prensa*, San Antonio 13 November 1914: 3; 15 November 1914: 3.

24. Interview with Sr. Cano Lucchese, San Antonio, May 1981. The family enterprise in shoe-making and real estate dates back to before 1910.

25. Promptbook 129, "La Mancha de Sangre," Hernández-Villalongín Collection in the Mexican American Collection at The University of Texas at Austin.

26. Interview with Sra. Villalongín de Santos. See John W. Brokaw, "A Mexican American Acting Company: 1849-1924," *Educational Theatre Journal* 27 (1975) 25-27.

27. *La Prensa* 13 January 1915. At the Teatro Zaragoza the theatre owner's daughters generally performed during the intermissions. Josephine Lucchese, who later became a renowned Metropolitan Opera star, sang to the accompaniment of her sister, María, at the piano.

28. Promptbook of "Benito Juárez," in private collection of Sra. Villalongín de Santos: 1.

29. *La Prensa* 27 December 1917: 5.

30. *La Prensa* 17 March 1915; 22 November 1914: 5-6; 26 November 1914: 6; *La Crónica*, Laredo 24 September 1911: 1.

31. Brockett 522-525. Jack Poggi, *Theatre in America: The Impact of Economic Forces, 1870-1967* (Ithaca, New York: Cornell University Press, 1968) 43-44.

32. Elizabeth C. Ramírez, "Spanish-language Combination Companies on the American Stage: Organization and Practice in Texas, 1915-1935," *Theatre History Studies* 1989.

33. *Las Noticias*, El Paso 23 December 1899: 2.

34. *Evolución* 11 December 1917: 1; 17 December 1917: 2; 26 December 1917: 1.

35. *La Prensa* 2 May 1928: 6.

36. Interview with Sr. Lalo Astol. "Memoirs of Lalo Astol," Mexican American Library Collection at The University of Texas at Austin.

37. *La Prensa* 20 November 1917: 5.

38. Rodolfo Usigli, *Mexico in the Theatre*, Trans., Wilder P. Scott (University of Mississippi: Romance Monographs, Inc., 1975) 110-111.

39. Brokaw 28. *La Prensa* 26 March 1923: l; 28 March 1923: l; 9 December 1926: 5, 10.

40. *Evolución* 2 June 1917: 2; 7 December 1917: 2.

41. *La Prensa* 5 August 1917: 5; *Evolución* 27 February 1919; *El Demócrata Fronterizo* 15 March 1919: l.

42. *La Prensa* 19 December 1917: 5.

43. Brockett 583-584; Poggi 28, 45, 87.

Chapter IV

The Production

In any period or culture reviewers are usually limited in their observations about production elements, namely, the scenery, costumes, lights, and the acting. Accounts dealing with productions by Spanish-language companies provide only general comments about the scenery, costumes, and lights. Of such accounts, the following three are typical in regard to these visual aspects of the production:

> The company [Compañía de la Lastra] brought all that was necessary to present a complete, majestic, and surprising performance.

> The staging [by the Compañía Villalongín] was well presented and well arranged with all the scenic changes greatly effective.

> The play [by the Compañía Virginia Fábregas] was staged with true luxury and appropriateness, both in respect to the scenery and to the costumes.[1]

We can gain some knowledge of these matters from other sources. Certain persons set the standard in costume and scenery for everyone, the most important of which were the leading actors of Spain, María Guerrero (1868-1928) and her husband, Fernando Díaz de Mendoza (1862-1930). Oscar G. Brockett, in his *History of the Theatre*, refers to these actors as the major Spanish actors of the modern period--1875-1915. Many well-known dramatists, such as Jacinto Benavente and the Álvarez Quintero brothers, wrote plays as vehicles for these actors. They managed the Teatro Espagñol (formerly the Teatro Príncipe) from 1896 to 1909, and from 1909 until 1924 the Teatro de la Princesa which was later renamed the Teatro María Guerrero. The Guerrero-Díaz de Mendoza company toured South America twenty-two times and elsewhere less often.[2]

Luis Reyes de la Maza, in his history of Mexican theatre, tells us that upon their first visit to Mexico in 1900, the Compañía Guerrero-Díaz de Mendoza:

> consisted of thirty-two actors, three prompters, a representative, a manager, an accountant, and the scenography for each and every one of the plays in their extensive repertory carefully packed as they travelled throughout the world. Sra. Guerrero's costumes filled twelve trunks and those of Don Fernando five, along with some dozens more for the rest of the actors. The company travelled throughout Hispanoamerica in that manner.[3]

The Compañía Guerrero-Díaz de Mendoza appeared again in Mexico in 1902, 1907, and 1921.

In 1926, *La Prensa* ran a front page article about María Guerrero announcing her upcoming appearance in the United States scheduled to begin on 6 January 1927. The tour was under the direction of Walter O. Lindsey. The company had been absent from the Madrid stage for two years, having been on an extensive tour of Central and South America during that time. The company had appeared in New York in May of 1926.[4]

In 1927, while on a long Latin American tour expected to end in San Francisco, the company appeared in Mexico City. Upon hearing of the activity in Texas, however, they booked an appearance at the Municipal Auditorium in San Antonio. This auditorium was the center of all theatrical and cultural activity primarily geared toward the English-language Anglo American community. They made their only known appearance in the Southwestern United States in San Antonio, Texas, in January of 1927 where they found a surprisingly large audience for Spanish-speaking theatre. The unexpected popularity and demand from the entire community made the company not only cancel their trip to San Francisco, but they remained in San Antonio for several performances. Sam Lucchese booked them at the Teatro Nacional for four more performances. By that time the Teatro Nacional was the center of Spanish-language entertainment. Thereafter, the company decided to return to Mexico City, instead of continuing on to San Francisco. They did, however, make a brief appearance in Laredo and Monterrey, Mexico, along the way.[5]

There is no question that the Compañía Guerrero-Díaz de Mendoza was a great influence on the practice and performance of Mexican companies. Reyes de la Maza calls María Guerrero the "actress of her time," and the Spanish-language theatre equalled her only to Sarah Bernhardt and Eleanora Duse. The appearance of her company in San Antonio clearly influenced Mexican American performers as well. It is obvious from his "Memoirs" that Carlo Villalongín was impressed by these Spanish artists. Clippings of stories about the two actors when they appeared in Texas and other clippings from Mexico were often referred to by Villalongín in his production planning.[6]

Authenticity and elegance were important factors in costuming for it was assumed that the great stars would represent both. María Luisa Villalongín de Santos, an actress in Carlos Villalongín's company for many years, recalls that her father often referred to photographs of renowned actors in an attempt not only to emulate them but also to present the characters in costumes true to the period in which they appeared. Companies sought to be as accurate as possible in costumes; accounts often informed the public that companies would provide "appropriate" costume for each play. The term "appropriate" suggests not only that the costumes were both proper and up to the standards of the company since the term appears in paid advertisements but also that newspaper critics used it as a standard in making judgments.

Most often the costume worn on stage was ordinary modern dress typical of the period. However, since many of the more frequently performed plays were period plays, something other than ordinary contemporary clothing had to be used for them or else audiences would not have been satisfied. Sr. Lalo Astol, who travelled with and worked with many of the larger companies in both Mexico and Texas, recalls that performers always dressed according to the demands of the production and period costumes were worn by actors when the need arose. More often than not, however, he along with other actors was expected to own and maintain the best in contemporary clothing, thus always having to keep up with changing fashion.

A few photographs are available of costumes worn by actors in Mexico prior to 1911 and others in Texas after 1911. From these pictures we may gather certain facts about the costume practice of Mexican American actors. One illustration is taken from a Mexican theatre bulletin in the Villalongín Collection at The University of Texas at Austin. The bulletin contains several illustrations of clothing of the period worn by actors. Illustration III reveals the "Fin de Siecle" style in clothing for both men and women typical for light romantic roles. This illustration is one of several that show that women dressed more extravagantly than men.

As to the men, the available illustrations suggest that there was little variety in male contemporary dress. One photograph shows the leading actor, Manuel Cotera, wearing a period costume that would be appropriate for roles such as Sebastián, the rancher and landowner in *Tierra baja*. (See Illustration IV.) Such attire would be especially appropriate for the son of Doña Sacramento, the young gallant, in *El genio alegre*, as would that seen in the photograph of A. de la Paz in Illustration V.

Great attention was given to the costumes. All actors maintained their own costumes, but comic actors had to devote extra attention to their wardrobe. Sr. Lalo Astol kept a box of wigs, make-up, and special properties needed for the varying business typically required of such actors. Although he was known to have performed in both comic and serious roles, after 1935 he specialized increasingly in popular comic sketches.

Besides the Villalongín children, other children of actors also appeared. In Illustration VI we can see the young Leonardo G. Astol (later known as Lalo Astol) in a special card used to solicit sponsors for his benefit performance. One photograph shows young boys in period costumes. (See Illustration VII.)

As to the scenic elements, most reports reveal that companies produced lavish and elaborate productions. We know that the "magnificent Compañía Labrada y Flores brought good costumes and elegant scenery appropriate to the works that they presented" in Laredo, according to the account of 5 November 1904, and that the Compañía José Martínez de la Lastra would perform "with apparatus and changes of scenery along with lavish costumes," for their engagement in Laredo in February 1906. On 28 April 1906 the Compañía Martínez de la Lastra was credited with presenting "a grand drama with both machinery and magic" in its production. In September 1907 the Teatro Solórzano advertised that all works were performed with "luxurious scenery and special costumes," but no specific details were provided. The performances of the Compañía Ricardo de la Vega in San Antonio in 1916 were advertised in such general terms as performances "with beautiful scenery" or indicating the number of scenic changes that would be shown. On the whole, performances were said to be "appropriately mounted with both costumes and scenery," as in the account of 5 April 1916 for the performances of the Compañía María del Carmen Martínez in San Antonio.[7]

The larger companies do provide us with a few more hints about scenery. In the account of 15 May 1915, the Compañía María del Carmen Martínez produced *La venganza de la Gleba* (Vengeance of the Glebe) on a stage that was described as "serious, intense, and adorned with realism torn from Zola." Their advertisement of 1918 indicated that they would produce *La plegaria de los náufragos* (The Supplication of the Shipwrecked), a "grand drama of grand apparatus," including "irons and snowcaps in full view of the public."[8]

About the Compañía Virginia Fábregas, *La Prensa* announced that "we have sources that tell us that the scenic properties with which their works will be presented constitute a new element of success," for the company. Such an announcement leaves much to the imagination, for the paper reported nothing more about scenic matters. In a later account, the Compañía Fábregas was reportedly appearing with the scenic properties "with which we have always seen it present its work."[9]

In Mexico painted backdrops were more common than set pieces and built-up scenery. Similar practice is evident on the

Mexican American stage. Illustration VIII shows one example of a backdrop used during a performance. Generally every act of a full-length drama was accompanied by at least one appropriate backdrop and these changed for every act. One reporter previewed the scenery for the benefit performance for the actor-manager Don Ricardo de la Vega at the Teatro Zaragoza in 1914. The account indicated that there was nothing left to be desired in terms of the scenery, for it not only included brilliant coloring in perspective, but "one had to add the magnificent scenic combination of furnishings and costumes that will be present." The theatre management had apparently supplied the costly elements, sparing no extravagance for the occasion. In order to let the public know what splendor to expect, the management had set up a display of seven photographs in the portico of the theatre showing the scenery and decorations for each of the seven acts of the drama *La abadía de Castro* (The Abbey of Castro).[10]

We know that a front curtain was used as evidenced by the frequent promptbook notations "P.T." or "Ready Curtain" (*Prepare Telón*) and "E.T." or "Curtain" (*Entre Telón*). Such notations are generally found at the beginning and end of each act. Almost all companies were reported in the press to be travelling with appropriate settings and effects but often the theatres in which they appeared could not accommodate all that they brought with them. The performances of the Compañía María del Carmen Martínez performing at the Teatro Juárez of San Antonio were "appropriately mounted in terms of costume but due to the small stage, their scenery was necessarily minimal."[11]

There are a few companies that distinguished themselves in terms of their spectacular productions. The Compañía Ricardo de la Vega produced many elaborate spectacles during its lengthy stay in San Antonio and subsequent tours. The company was highly praised for its "extravagant machines, scenic changes, and scenery." *Don Juan Tenorio*, a drama with unusually demanding scenic changes, was often evaluated in terms of whether the production was presented with the necessary scenery the drama required. Ghosts, moving statues, shadows appearing through walls, and the opening of a sepulchre in a cemetery where all the buried dead begin to walk are among the many scenic demands. This drama was produced so often that there was often much with which it could be compared. In the paid advertisement for the Teatro Salon Lincoln in Laredo, the performance announced on 29 July 1918 indicated that *Don Juan Tenorio* would be presented with "special costumes along with transformations and apparitions in full view of the audience."[12]

Probably the most elaborate of all companies to appear in Texas was the Compañía Fábregas. The public knew they could expect the very best in theatrical production from this company since the newspapers always kept everyone abreast of what the famous actress had to offer, both in Mexico and abroad. Generally, the Compañía Fábregas was announced to be expected far in advance, always promising the public new scenery for its productions and both audiences and reviewers were never disappointed.

There is little available information about lighting. The auditorium was dark while the stage was lit at least by 1910. Sr. Astol and Sra. Villalongín de Santos recall from the earliest performances they witnessed on Texas stages as well as their own experience on the stage that lighting came from above and from footlights. Yet, it is impossible to know what may have occurred prior to 1915 since no accounts reveal matters about lighting on the stage. Prior to 1900 the lighting equipment was probably not electric; hence, candles were probably used. In Mexico, prior to electricity, "Quinques" or kerosene lamps were used because they were less expensive than candles. We do know that by 1915 electricity was installed at the Teatro Zaragoza in San Antonio which would indicate that electric lighting was in use at least by then. Both the Teatro Zaragoza and later the Teatro Nacional were always reported to be the most modern of theatres and generally the management was quick to make the necessary innovations to keep these theatres up to date with the latest innovations by Mexico City standards.

The little attention given to the production elements in newspaper reviews and accounts of the performance indicates a focus on the actor. It is clear that the actors dominated the performance and thus the most informative accounts concern actors and acting.

The twentieth century brought a great many Spanish-language dramatic actors to Texas. The first quarter of the twentieth century witnessed a significant movement in theatrical entertainment which included a variety of dramatic performances. In these performances extant reviews reveal the value reviewers placed on the plays themselves. Accounts of the performances primarily emphasized the plays and especially their didactic and moralistic merits. The principal performers were generally noted for their accomplishments on the stage in conveying the full understanding of the play. The performers not only acquainted audiences with traditional and innovative drama, but they often set the standard in language, customs and manners, and in fashion.

The most numerous accounts available on an actress performing prior to 1900 are about Antonia Pineda de Hernández (?-c.1927). (See Illustration IX.) At the age of 18 she married Encarnación Hernández whom she met when he was performing in a company with Francisco Solórzano in Colima, Mexico. Her father was of Italian origin and her mother Spanish, and neither had a theatrical background. Hernández trained her as an actress according to her descendants. She eventually became the leading actress of the company that Encarnación organized, the Compañía Hernández. Upon her husband's death (c.1888), she assumed responsibility of company management which she continued until her retirement in 1904 when Carlos Villalongín, her son-in-law, took over the management. She also continued as leading actress to Carlos Villalongín. Her children included one son, Luis, who acted with the company, and two daughters that became actresses in the Hernández-Villalongín company and later the Compañía Villalongín. Herlinda, who generally performed in various second-line parts, married Carlos Villalongín, and Concepción assumed the leading role when she could fill the part and as her mother took on fewer or smaller roles and eventually retired. Antonia Pineda de Hernández was best known for her roles in romantic tragedy and melodramas. Her last known performance was as the leading actress in

La campa de la mudaña for a benefit event at Beethoven Hall in San Antonio in 1917.

The peak of Antonia Pineda de Hernández's career as an actress was prior to 1900. There are other actresses about which we know more and can stand out as good examples of the type of performers that appeared in the touring and resident companies after 1900. Three actresses stand out as particularly powerful figures on the Mexican American stage in Texas between 1900 and 1915, namely, Magdalena Solórzano, Margarita Fernández, and Concepción Hernández. Since these three women performed in more or less the same style, it is possible to select one as representative.

In Concepción Hernández we have an excellent example of the type of leading actress commonly found in the Mexican touring companies that appeared in Texas. Srta. Hernández is additionally important because she also is representative of the type of actress that remained in Texas to continue the theatrical tradition through the resident company.

Extant photographs of Srta. Hernández show a figure rather stocky but very straight in posture. (See Illustration X.) We know that she was of average height, a few inches over five feet tall, the approximate height of her leading man. She seemed older than her age, a quality common in women in their early twenties of that period, and thus she was probably well suited to play opposite Carlos Villalongín, who had grayed prematurely.

The features most often written about by newspaper critics were an actress' intelligence, ability to comprehend her part, and skill in presenting a well-studied role with clarity in diction--all of which were accomplished by Srta. Hernández according to extant accounts. Her principal strength, however, was a unique vocal range. A vivid description remains of her most memorable role, that of Marta in *Tierra baja*; Carlos Villalongín included in his memoirs the newspaper review of the performance of 20 February 1910 in Matamoros, Mexico. This review is important because it provides an account of one of the Compañía Villalongín's productions known to have been presented in San Antonio. In this performance, Concepción Hernández is said to have been "truly inspired" and to have "painted with vivid colors all the sufferings of that sublime martyr of disgrace." The account continues:

> Her potent voice ranged from a ferocious roar of injured dignity; to the soft
> cooing and billing of a dove, sweet and harmonious, as a murmur of breezes
> from the fjords, when, for the first time, she felt the beating in her heart of
> the sweet sensations of true love. [13]

Her most outstanding feature was her powerful and wide-ranging voice, which she used with great skill in conveying emotion:

> All her inflections imprinted a stamp of truth to the different sensations of
> hate, indignation, dignity, contempt, passion and tenderness with which the
> difficult role of Marta is filled; in all of those transitions, this singular artist
> knew how to triumph, receiving for it merited ovations.

About all the other actors it was reported that they "in general, made a conscious performance second only to that of the two principal figures of the drama," Marta and Manelich (Carlos Villalongín played the part of Manelich to Concepción Hernández' Marta.)

The manners of the period required that the declamatory actress perform in moral and instructive dramas suitable for the entire family. The fact that Concepción Hernández was performing in a family enterprise, always accompanied by her mother, sisters, and other relatives probably enhanced the image of wholesome entertainment that the Compañía Villalongín provided. Rarely was she regarded as beautiful but her performances were valued for other reasons.

Srta. Hernández' training began in childhood and she grew into the parts she played. Her parents were actors and managers of the Compañía Hernández prior to its merger with the Compañía Villalongín. In later years Concepción would have had to share roles with her sister, Herlinda, but upon her marriage Herlinda turned her attention to other matters, such as taking care of the nine children she bore. Thus, Concepción was almost exclusively the leading lady of the company. Among her principal roles were the already mentioned Marta in *Tierra baja*, *María Antonietta*, *La llorona*, and Doña Ines in *Don Juan Tenorio*.

Concepción Hernández received many gifts, special notes, poems, and pictures from people offering friendship and other tokens of admiration. Examples of some of these are found in the Villalongín Collection, such as cards and photographs from admirers, generally wishing her successful benefit performances. Carlos Villalongín's "Memoirs" also include a poem written to Concepción prior to her permanent stay in San Antonio. Although some of the sentiment may be lost in translation, from this poem we get a glimpse of the unique qualities this artist possessed:

> To the Inspired Mexican Artist, Srta. Concepción Hernández at her benefit performance:
>
> My lips always burst out in praise for all that shone or consoled; that is why I want to pay tribute to the faithful interpreter of melodrama.
>
> The inspiration of your creations is born in your soul; and you lovingly make it [the melodrama] live in the hearts of everyone. You create a reality of both suffering and feeling. Your modesty is a gift! A gift of art! You have arrived at the summit without faltering. From that height, the resplendent torch of progress will make you shine. Continue receiving applause in your art, the prize for your difficult labors; you move everyone's soul; in your path flowers are strewn.
>
> If your life, O Concha [short name of endearment for Concepción], encounters paths of thistles and thorns, remember, beautiful lady of the border, that a heart remains for you here in Sabinas.
>
> > Fidencio M. Chinauya [spelling unclear]
> > Sabinas Hidalgo, Mexico, 9 April 1911[14]

Not long after those words were written the actress found herself in San Antonio where the company performed at the Teatro Aurora.

Other actresses were significant for their changing style of acting and introduction of new roles. Virginia Fábregas probably best represents the "modern actress," although there are other examples such as Mercedes Navarro and Rosita Arriaga.

Virginia Fábregas has been described as demure, delicate, and light in her performances on stage. As Rodolfo Usigli states: "She is the first actress with vision, not of what the theatre was then [in the last decade of the 19th century] but of what it would be later, and consequently, she is the first modern actress of Mexico." She not only educated the public, but as she has stated, she "learned as well." Probably her most outstanding attribute was her ability to portray emotion and feel the part in a performance but in a unique and thoroughly natural and believable manner.[15]

Virginia Fábregas made her stage debut on 30 April 1892 at the Teatro Principal in Mexico City. She appeared in *Divorciemonos* (although the playwright is unknown, this is probably a translation of Sardou's *Divorcous*) as the ingenue (*dama joven*). She captivated the audience with her beauty but not the theatre critics. They were bothered by her inadequate analysis of her role without taking into account the fact that her performance was accompanied by the nervousness generally found in young actresses. Later in life she would often refer to these as the "first thorns of many more" she would be injured by, as she ascended the road to fame and glory.[16]

Virginia Fábregas was born in Yautepec in the State of Morelos, in 1872, and was taken to Campeche as a young child (located in the Yucatan Peninsula). Being orphaned, she had to work for a living from the age of 12, entering as an aide at the School for Deaf-mutes where she received scant wages. Driven by her artistic inclinations and looking for a wider field in which to attain her aspirations, she decided to dedicate herself to the theatre. Making her first public appearance at the Teatro Principal as an amateur, she recited the monologue of Eduardo Noriega in *La primera carta* (The First Letter) and later acted in a few benefits (*festival de caridad*) until she was engaged by a professional dramatic company. From then on to her death she triumphed, even being honored with the decoration of the Palmas Académicas by the government of France.

No individual star had a greater influence on play production than Virginia Fábregas both on the Mexican stage and the Mexican American stage in Texas. We have already discovered many facts about this actress and her company. About her repertory we know that she was internationally acclaimed in *La mujer x* and that her portrayal of Angélica in *La hija del rey* [mentioned in the discussion on repertory], was significant in the revival of romanticism in Mexico. She later turned to plays by modern dramatists with much enthusiasm, believing that to present drama with universal appeal, capable of reaching the widest possible audience was the greatest accomplishment of any performer.

About the men, we of course know most about Carlos Villalongín, but it is safe to say that as an actor he resembled Francisco E. Solórzano, José Martínez de la Lastra, and Ricardo de la Vega. Francisco E. Solórzano's experience and well-known success on the Mexican stage in management and as a performer was so vast and dated back to such an early time that his association with Carlos Villalongín as both came to settle in Texas probably did much to inform the latter in many respects.

On the stage, Carlos Villalongín did not receive the same degree of tribute and attention given Concepción Hernández in the review of *Tierra baja* quoted earlier. In it, his role as Manelich is described as that of "a rustic, almost savage man, with the strength of a beast and the heart of a child." The character of Manelich as portrayed by Villalongín was dominated only by the sweet voice of a woman." The reviewer noted that "all of this Sr. Villalongín knew how to interpret," and "together with Srta. Hernández, the artistic triumph that they won was in twice being warmly called back to the stage." (See Illustration XI.)[17]

Most reviews in which Sr. Villalongín's portrayal is discussed are brief since they primarily center on the leading lady's performance. Generally, however, commentary about his performance was favorable, for he was said either to be able to "sustain" the character throughout the performance with "much skill in his art," or to be able to show that he knew what he had "within his hands," for the characters he played were admirable. He was called a "modest, unequalled, and handsome artist." The criteria used to evaluate a good actor was generally his capacity to comprehend his part and portray emotion, but, above all, not to detract from the sentiment and emotion displayed by the actress. Villalongín did receive acclaim, but due to the many responsibilities he had to assume within the company, he did not become a major star.[18]

Manuel Cotera is an excellent example of the young male actor that remained in Texas for a long time. Cotera first appeared in Texas in 1918 as the leading actor in the Compañía María del Carmen Martínez. By 1920 he was again touring in Texas but with his own company. He toured often within the State, often featuring (when available) Concepción Hernández and subsequently her niece, María Luisa Villalongín who had by then grown into the parts her aunt had once played.[19]

The numerous accounts about Cotera reveal that he was handsome, had a great appeal with young women in the audience, and was considered a "fine and elegant artist." Illustration IV clearly shows a dashing figure in Cotera. In one account of his performance at the Teatro Nacional he was Armand to María Luisa Villalongín's Margarita in *La dama de las camelias* (Camille) and although the reviewer wondered why he did not shoot himself upon seeing the cadaver of the beautiful Margarita played so "ideally" by the young actress, he was nevertheless praised for his performance.[20]

Besides his accomplishments as an actor, Cotera also ventured into company management and even playwriting. Obviously, due to a lack of new works available, Cotera began to adapt plays. An account of 5 March 1923 praises his adaptation of *Mavis*, in which he had taken one of the best works by the renowned Spanish writer Felipe Trigo and made it into an interesting and passionate work. The reviewer stated that Cotera had revealed himself "well able to recognize the secrets of the theatre," for he was able to place various theatrical punches" to produce the desired effects on the audience, and the work "constituted a legitimate triumph" for Cotera.[21]

Among the comic actors that appeared on the Mexican American stage, several notable figures can be considered representative of the type. All of the more popular comic actors had particular distinguishing features that made them stand out among others performing in that genre. We are fortunate enough to have accounts of certain actors who were particularly well-known in Texas.

Mariano Villalongín headed his own "cuadro de zarzuela y comedia," a group that toured in northern Mexico and eventually arrived in Texas where this comic actor took up residence in San Antonio. (See Illustration VIII.) The distinguishing feature of this actor was his limited height. Carlos Villalongín's memoirs give us a clue to this with a brief poem that appeared in a newspaper which is entitled "Crecio Mucho" or "He Grew Alot." Although it is only partly legible, we find that Mariano Villalongín was: "Half a foot in height/[But] Now he is even taller than Pirrimplin/because he drinks aspirin/in the Restaurant of "El _____." Apparently this was an endorsement both of a product and a local restaurant in a town where Villalongín was performing. He was also called the "actor cómico el chaparrito," meaning the short comic actor. He often had the leading role in comic parts with dramatic companies, as for example with the Compañía de Drama, Comedia y Variedad González Rada at the Teatro Juárez in Laredo, Texas. He did, however, also play serious roles, as evidenced by his performance in Dumas' *El Conde de Monte-Cristo* at the Teatro Juárez.

In one review for his benefit performance, Mariano Villalongín is said to be "one of the actors that is more loved by the audience where he has performed because of his original comic details; he knows how to leave the public favorably impressed with his performances." The Compañía Azteca which he managed included at least nine actors plus a musical band and the orchestra quartet "Neoleones," all of whom travelled with the company.[22] Mariano Villalongín eventually returned to Mexico toward the end of his life where he died in Coahuila.

Leonardo G. Astol became a well-known actor of both serious and comic genres in San Antonio. (See Illustration XII.) Sr. Astol, better known today as Lalo Astol, began his career as a child actor touring with his mother's dramatic company in Mexico and eventually came to reside in Laredo with his father. After the Compañía Azteca (different from the one of that name headed by Mariano Villalongín) was formed by his father, Lalo Astol toured with the company, growing into parts as they became available and as he grew older. Comic roles were particularly suited to him, sharing Mariano Villalongín's shortness in stature. To him is attributed the long tradition of variety sketches in Spanish which became popular forms of entertainment beginning in the late twenties, and he later performed on radio and eventually television.

Probably the most popular comic actor for the longest period of time was Arturo García Pajujo. Many individuals in San Antonio and elsewhere in Texas still recall this actor. Of Spanish origin, he had gained prominence on the Mexican stage by 1910, and by 1915 had already appeared in Texas several times and continued to do so for many years afterward. He never settled permanently in Texas, although he and his family stayed in San Antonio for extended periods. His wife came from a family long established in the theatre in Mexico. His sisters-in-law were María del Carmen Martínez and María del Pilar Martínez, both of whom had their own touring companies, and the first of whom was a leading actress on the stage of Mexico City. It was customary for Pajujo, as this actor was usually called, and his wife to stay in the Carlos Villalongín home when they were engaged in San Antonio. For a time Pajujo directed a company in which Carlos Villalongín and Concepción Hernández were the leading actors and in which his wife, María Martínez, performed as well, with Pajujo starring in the comic short pieces which followed the full-length plays.

The Villalongín Collection (through extant broadsides, theatre bulletins, pictures and other memorabilia) shows Pajujo's prominence as an actor. Some accounts are especially entertaining in announcements of his performances or those of his company. His great friendship with the editors of *La Prensa* led him in 1914 to contrive a benefit performance for them which gave him much publicity. He was said to have been the victim of a great caper in which someone had run over his "very long, prominent nose!" In Illustration XIII we can view a caricature of Pajujo in which his unique feature is emphasized. Not only is his nose overextended, but we can also note his unusual attire. The caricature appeared in a newspaper which he published in preparation for one of his performances in Monterrey, Mexico, in 1909, and it is filled with many examples to show his ability to concoct a variety of antics (The subtitle indicates this is a paid advertisement or broadside.).

Through the extant newspaper reviews and accounts of the performances by the Spanish-language professional dramatic companies in Texas we can see that the little attention given to the production elements was due to the focus on the actor. Costumes, scenery, and lighting were necessary for the effectiveness of each production, but the importance of the actor's performance was highlighted. The actor was expected to evoke high moral standards, show close family unity, and provide well-studied parts. Above all else, however, the actor was evaluated for his vocal range and intensity, clarity in speech, and display of high emotions. It is clear that the actors dominated the performance, and other production elements, if they did not eclipse them, did not normally detract from their performances either. Clearly the performers held the focus of attention for their audiences and were regarded with high esteem in the community.

Notes

1. *El Demócrata Fronterizo*, Laredo 21 April 1906:3; "Memoirs of Carlos Villalongín," in the private collection of Sra. María Luisa Villalongín de Santos, San Antonio, Texas; *La Prensa*, San Antonio 21 November 1926: 5.

2. Oscar G. Brockett, *History of the Theatre*, 3rd ed. (New York: Allyn and Bacon, Inc., 1977) 496.

3. Luis Reyes de la Maza, *El teatro en México* (Mexico: U.N.A.M., 1953-1970) 1900-1910: 9-10.

4. *La Prensa*, San Antonio 21 November 1926: 5, 7; 28 December 1926: 10; 31 December 1926: 10; 6 January 1927: 5, 6; 13 January 1927: 4.

5. *La Prensa* 23 January 1927: 8.

6. Reyes de la Maza 9, 33; "Memoirs of Carlos Villalongín."

7. *El Demócrata Fronterizo*, 5 November 1904: 1; 17 February 1906: 2; 28 April 1906; 21 September 1907: 2; *La Prensa* 19 November 1914: 6; 27 November 1914: 6; 5 December 1914: 6; 5 April 1916: 5.

8. *La Prensa* 15 May 1916: 5; 3 December 1917: 5; 14 August 1918.

9. *La Prensa* 16 December 1917: 5.

10. *La Prensa* 18 November 1914: 6.

11. *La Prensa* 5 April 1916: 5.

12. *Evolución*, Laredo 29 July 1918: 3.

13. "Memoirs of Carlos Villalongín," 96, 108, 123.

14. "Memoirs of Carlos Villalongín," 100.

15. Rodolfo Usigli, *Mexico in the Theatre*, Trans. Wilder E. Scott (University of Mississippi: Romance Monographs, Inc., 1975) 18: 110; *La Prensa* 4 April 1923: 5; 25 November 1926: 5; 28 November 1926: 1; 2 May 1928: 6, 9.

16. Manuel Mañon, *Historia del Teatro Principal de México* (Mexico: Editorial Cultura, 1932) 152.

17. "Memoirs of Carlos Villalongín," 95-96.

18. "Memoirs of Carlos Villalongín," 92.

19. *La Prensa* 2 April 1916: 5; *El Demócrata Fronterizo* 25 May 1918: 3; 13 July 1918: 4; *La Patria*, El Paso 8 June 1920: 3; 13 June 1920: 4; 24 July 1920: 2.

20. "Memoirs of Carlos Villalongín," 121.

21. *La Prensa* 5 March 1923: 8.

22. "Memoirs of Carlos Villalongín," 179, 184-186.

Chapter V

Audiences and Performances

In Ricardo Romo's "The Urbanization of Southwestern Chicanos in the Early Twentieth Century," we learn that the population of the Southwest grew slowly during the late nineteenth and early twentieth century as it attracted only a small number of European immigrants and other migrants. Arnoldo De Leon has done extensive research on *The Tejano Community*, which focuses on the period between 1836 and 1900 and reveals much about the urban and rural experience of the Mexican American people during that time. However, the larger cities like San Antonio and El Paso did not experience rapid urbanization until after 1900 and it was in the 1900-1930 era that these cities attracted Mexican Americans in record numbers. Due to a diversified economic structure, closeness to the Mexican border and good prospects for employment, the urban areas attracted large numbers of Mexicans to Texas.[1]

A larger number of Mexicans settled in Texas than in the other states. Between 1900 and 1920 the percentage of Mexican migrants going across the border was 70% heading for Texas and initially only 6.5% going to California. In 1920 San Antonio had a distribution of 41,469 Mexican Americans, and 82,373 in 1930. El Paso had 39,571 in 1920 and 58,291 in 1930. Data for Laredo is unavailable for 1920, but in 1930 there were 23,482. Houston had only 5002 in 1920 and 14,149 in 1930; Dallas 2,838 in 1920 and 5,901 in 1930; Austin (data unavailable for 1920), 5,014 in 1930; and Corpus Christi (unavailable for 1920), 11,377 in 1930. Accuracy in census count for Mexicans in these areas has been disputed by some. Yet, clearly, by 1920 urban areas contained unusually large numbers of Mexicans.[2]

San Antonio and El Paso rapidly gained substantially in population due to excellent rail connections, lower prices in fuel for industrialization and ready access to a continuing supply of Mexican labor. The regional markets in West Texas and South Texas were not as promising as El Paso and San Antonio in terms of commerce and shipping of raw resources. Carey McWilliams points out that the Lower Rio Grande Valley was retarded by a hundred years of border warfare and its economic development did not get underway until the completion of the St. Louis-Brownsville-Mexican rail line in 1904. The economy of El Paso, however, was quite diversified and by 1900 San Antonio was the largest city in the State situated in the axis of a major agricultural and cattle raising area in South and Central Texas.

The rapid urbanization of San Antonio in the post 1910 era was related to the building of several military bases in the edges of the city by the federal government. The bases meant more jobs during World War I, and after the war San Antonio kept its position as a major commercial center in South Texas due to improved transportation facilities.

San Antonio stands out as particularly affected by the emigration of Mexicans from Mexico during the years of civil war in that country. In all the bigger cities in Texas, the large influx of exiled and political refugees helped to establish a growing upper class of Mexican Americans, and by the end of the first quarter of the twentieth century a growing middle class was becoming evident. However, it is significant that from 1890 to 1920, San Antonio had the largest concentration of Mexican Americans in the United States with 53,321 in a total population of 161,379.[3]

The types of jobs Spanish-speaking people held were varied. We find that prior to 1910 the majority of Mexican Americans labored outside the urban and industrial job market. But as economic opportunities improved in cities like San Antonio and Houston, the Mexican American labor forces migrated less frequently to distant agricultural areas, more and more working at factories, foundries, and construction jobs. The greater number of Mexican Americans held jobs as laborers. Many worked in semi-skilled and skilled jobs as carpenters, tailors, painters, and bakers. In El Paso, more and more service jobs were becoming available between 1900 and 1920, and in San Antonio some even worked for the city in unskilled and semi-skilled jobs and there were even storekeepers and clerks.

The larger urban areas understandably provide us with more information about the period under study here. It was these areas that generally attracted the Spanish-language dramatic troupes in Texas. One of the reasons for the very favorable reception and high success of the dramatic companies was that entertainment on the whole in the Spanish-language community was severely lacking until the first decade of the 20th century. The people were still starved for cultural entertainment as they had been prior to 1900 and the growing population made the demand even more profound.

Entertainment primarily consisted of civic functions organized by patriotic committees centered around official celebrations such as centennial celebrations, significant local historical events, and especially the 16th of September, commemorating Mexico's independence from Spain. In Bejar County (which included San Antonio) and in El Paso, these types of festivities were generally extensive, drawing many people from surrounding communities to attend several days of events.

Religious holidays were also celebrated and the people often partook in organizing events that included amateur productions of popular plays, poetry readings and recitations. In an account of 1905 in Laredo, the festivities of Corpus Christi included an amateur production of "Romeo y Julieta" which was fully attended and greatly applauded by a public desirous of theatrical diversion. Other forms of entertainment included cockfights, dances, and *charreadas* (similar to rodeos). There were often serenades and bands playing in the plazas and parks. Although musical entertainment was more often found in individual homes, some clubs featured visiting singers from Italy, Spain, and Mexico en route from Mexico City. Italian opera, also travelling from the Capital, was popular although infrequent.[4]

Many immigrants in Texas joined clubs and societies that served to provide a collective force in both social and political matters. The noted Mexican anthropologist, Manuel Gamio, writing about *Mexican Immigration in the United States* in the 1920s, has commented on the popularity of the *sociedades mutualistas* or mutual benefit societies among the Mexicans in the United States. A variety of clubs and societies existed from which to choose and many of these did provide varying forms primarily of amateur entertainment.   In El Paso, Mexican Americans organized political clubs such as the *Club Ortiz Político Social* which succeeded in bringing many urban newcomers in contact with others of the same socio-economic background or similarities in ethnic background and traditions.   The *Orden Hijos de América* was an important organization that originated in San Antonio during the recession of 1921 when Mexicans were being faced with threats of deportation in San Antonio and elsewhere in the State.   All of these organizations were ways in which immigrants were able to fit in to a new way of life.[5]

These circumstances provide the setting in which the Spanish-language dramatic troupes appeared.   Diverse cultural entertainment was available, but theatrical entertainment was evidently in great demand.   Clearly the greater amount of dramatic activity occurred in the major Spanish-language population centers at the time.   These centers established various means of communication not only for their own inhabitants but to reach out-lying communities as well.   Spanish language newspapers informed about events in many surrounding communities but their major interests lay in announcing events in Mexico.   The smaller cities depended on the larger urban areas for that information.

El Demócrata Fronterizo was an early newspaper that did much to advertise activity and news for Spanish-speaking people but it was largely limited to Laredo.   Other newspapers soon followed. *La Prensa* was the largest and most significant Spanish-language newspaper in Texas.   This newspaper catered to a cosmopolitan population which was comprised of a very large group.   Many smaller newspapers such as *La Fe Católica* were church related and strived to maintain a close-knit, traditional and specific readership. A daily newspaper like *La Prensa*, however, was, in effect, serving a growing community. The Spanish-language community was so large in San Antonio that the newspaper there served many purposes. Advertisements for the large department stores like Joske's and many major and local merchants was common in *La Prensa* along with activities and entertainment for everyone. The newspaper's major focus was on the concerns of the Spanish-speaking population, but it was not restricted to that group. Often non-Hispanic concerns, activities, and advertisements appeared as well.

La Prensa began publishing at a time when Mexico was in the midst of its revolution. This newspaper evidently catered to the elite former members of the Díaz Regime from Mexico, for many of these most cultured individuals flocked to San Antonio for refuge. Yet, the reading public also included the educated classes who demanded to know all about activities in the United States, Europe, and Mexico, and the newspaper always strived to maintain the workingman's subscription as well. Fortunately for the theatre men such as the great Mexican General Urrutia, later a renowned surgeon, and Manuel Musquiz Blanco frequented the theatre. General Urrutia was said to have had his own box at the Teatro Nacional and always attended with his family in full dress uniform with many medals. Because the editors of *La Prensa* were comprised of many from the elite group of refugees, the theatre profited greatly from their interest. These powerful men in the Spanish-speaking community were used to attending cultural affairs and the theatre in Mexico, and the theatre continued to be high on their list of priorities as the tradition continued in San Antonio and other cities.

Among other sources, these Spanish-language newspapers show that the performers were much admired by their audiences. The reviewers evaluated actors on how well they did their job, and dealt in greatest detail with the plays. Above all other matters, the plays attracted the most attention in reviews. Thus, we can see through them the audience's interests in the actual performance witnessed on the Mexican American stage in Texas (See Illustration XIV.)

The theatrical season in the Spanish-language theatre in Texas differed from the Anglo theatre in that the first season began at the end of Holy Week, which might either be on Easter Sunday or shortly after that. This was also the usual practice in Mexico and in Spain. In Spain as late as 1919 the court theatres closed during the summer months. This was often the case in Texas as well since the theatres were not air-conditioned and few troupes were able to perform out of doors. Informants mention that although companies may have been resident in a major city through most of the year, it was not uncommon for them to tour during the summer months because the hot weather accompanied by poor ventilation led to uncomfortable conditions inside the theatres. Such conditions caused poor attendance in the theatres which led theatre managers to close their facilities through the summer. The resident companies were fortunate to find an eager audience throughout the Texas valley and did much touring during that time. The Texas valley (that is, south Texas along the Texas border between Rio Grande City and Brownsville, which included such cities as Mercedes, Donna, Pharr, and Mission) or the south central area (that is, the south central Texas cities which included San Diego, Benavides, and Hebbronville), were areas seldom frequented by the larger touring companies, a fact that led to such touring by the smaller companies. The arrival of new troupes with visiting stars from Mexico and Spain (which themselves had been left without theatres in which to perform during these months) led the smaller companies already residing in Texas to tour to those areas not frequented by the larger groups.

There is record of only one performance occurring on Christmas day or during the week between 25 December and 1 January. Theatres generally opened again sometime after 1 January. In 1915 the season at the Teatro Zaragoza in San Antonio began on 28 January and ended on 28 March, just prior to Holy Week. The season generally ended at the beginning of Holy Week and the new season would then again get underway after Easter Sunday. Although there were many variations in the practices described above there were no marked changes until after 1935.

We learn something about the audiences through their attendance at performances. The prices of admission varied greatly depending on the type of company performing. The rates, determined by the seating arrangement, indicate that different classes of people attended. Some companies charged much higher admission rates than others. The Compañía Fábregas probably charged more than any other company, with front-row seats (*lunetas*) at $1.00 (if reserved in advance, $1.50); and 25 cents and 50 cents in the galleries. These prices were for performances in 1917 and 1918; by 1920 increases were by about 25 cents to 50 cents in each section. The Compañía María del Carmen Martínez usually charged what they referred to as "greatly reduced prices," although we have no idea of what these were. If theatre admission rates were comparable to those for movie houses before 1920, they could have ranged from 10 cents to 25 cents. The prices for theatrical performances in El Paso in July of 1920 were: 50 cents, 30 cents, and 20 cents, plus a war tax (a practice begun after the first World War) of 5 cents to 10 cents. Prices did not vary, except for special performances or benefits, for which higher rates were charged. Tickets for matinee performances were almost always 5 cents and 10 cents. When unusually extravagant performances were given, companies charged higher rates, as for the performance of *Don Juan Tenorio* in Laredo in August of 1918. The Compañía María del Carmen Martínez performed this drama "al reves" or in reverse, with women doing men's parts and at the end the men dressed as "mariposas" or butterflies, doing a dance of that name.[6]

How did the people know about the performances? One of the reasons for the scant information now available on Spanish-language theatrical activity is that much of it was advertised by word of mouth, handbills, or broadsides. It was not until after 1915 that paid advertisements in newspapers became common. Resident companies were largely responsible for establishing that practice and *La Prensa* as well as the other extant newspapers show many paid advertisements.

Prior to 1915 many appeals were made in newspapers to the public asking them to patronize performances. These appeals are a

major source of information about the performances. The newspaper critics appear to reflect the taste, standards and biases of
Mexican Americans living in Texas in the early part of the twentieth century. From the critical articles we can glean the aesthetic,
social, and moral values of the age. The critics evaluated the actors
and the performances and reveal the effectiveness of performers
and performances.

The accounts which indicated the aesthetic values of the audiences were primarily those which mentioned the audiences' ap-
proval through great applause, generosity, and full-houses. The
productions were judged as of the greatest value if they were
well-known "grand" or "high Mexican dramas" and presented in
formal Spanish. In one account a dramatic company was praised
for "making us familiar with the treasures previous to the contemporary theatre in our mother tongue, that is, in the sweet and
melodious language of Cervantes," and "for only a few cents," one
can see the "exquisite emotions that dramatic art offers and the
portrayal of life in a prism of enchanted fiction through a drama or
comedia." From other accounts we learn that "above all," the companies were acclaimed for their "efforts" in bringing this dramatic
fare to the Texas audiences: "for these valuable artists place their
good-will, desires, eagerness, and their very souls in service for the
stage; they allow the public to experience the sensation of diverse
depictions of life and cultures."[7]

Certain accounts relate the social values of the theatre. In an account of 10 December 1904, the theatre in Laredo had trouble
drawing an audience to see one of the best acclaimed dramatic
companies from Mexico City. The reason for this was that the
company was competing with other social events such as the week
of fiestas and the local fair. By 1905, however, the accounts indicate that the theatre was providing a regular means of social entertainment and one which the public seemingly could not do without.
In 1906 a reporter in Laredo was very pleased to announce that
following a period of many festivities in February they were still
able to divert themselves with various forms of entertainment, not

the least of which was dramatic entertainment in two theatres in the city.[8]

The benefit performance for María del Carmen Martínez of 12 May 1916 was considered an event of "high culture," and the actress was commended by the newspaperman for coming to the Mexican people from Mexico and bringing the best of that country's art. At that function, the leading actress, Srta. Martínez, and the leading man, Sr. Manuel Cotera, were "showered with many gifts," and the newspaperman stated that "the homage paid to the actress must have impressed her for the audience was loving, spontaneous, and conscientious" in their reception of the company's performance. One newspaperman, Don Guillermo Aguirre y Fierro, read a poem at the benefit performance which he wrote expressly for that evening's performance. The actress in turn gave a final performance as a "función de gracias" or "event of gratitude" which she dedicated to the women, various honorable gentlemen, and to all of the local newspapers that published in Spanish. Such a dedication insured the company that the elite society would turn out for the event, especially since individuals were mentioned by name. This particular dedication and forthcoming event must have pleased the newspapermen greatly for they responded by publishing a large photograph of the leading actress in the newspaper which appeared the following day.[9]

In the account of 20 February 1918 in *La Prensa*, we learn that Sunday performances at least had become "worthwhile artistic and social events" at the Teatro Nacional, firmly established as part of the social entertainment provided by that city. The theatre manager, Sam Lucchese, was even including Josephine Lucchese, by then a renowned opera star, as a contracted performer to sing select arias between acts during some of these Sunday performances. In general, newspaper accounts were similar to that of 25 June 1917 of *La Prensa*, which stated that theatrical events brought the "distinguished Mexican society of San Antonio" to the theatre and it was referred to as a "select society" in such accounts. The account of 12 May 1916 called the benefit of María del Carmen Martínez a "success of high culture." On the whole, as the account of 30 January 1918 noted, the public "attends nightly, giving great applause" since the "Mexican public that spends on spectacles of culture has been greatly satisfied."[10]

The importance of displaying moral values in the dramas is revealed in several accounts. Informants who were acting with dramatic companies indicate that the intent of many directors was to educate the public through the plays they presented. Sra. María Luisa Villalongín de Santos states that her father always spoke to the company beforehand about the moral values of the drama he has chosen for performance and the importance of relating those values to the audience. She quotes him as referring to the theatre as a "Temple of Instruction," and it was up to the actors to do justice to each work in their interpretation. Sr. Lalo Astol, on the other hand, recalls reading the many lines of dialogue at the end of plays which his father often added to insure that audiences would clearly grasp the moral lessons to be gained through the dramas. There are many examples of lines added to the text in both the Hernández-Villalongín and the Astol collections of promptbooks, most of which appeared at the end, either paraphrasing the original, substituting it with a more contemporary interpretation, or reinforcing the central theme or ideas in the drama.

The account of 12 October 1907 states that the Catholic priest Augustín Rivera had been sent by the cultured society of Aguascalientes, Mexico, to address the Laredo public in behalf of the theatre as a means of gathering an audience as an assured measure of teaching the masses, "instructing them morally." In another account the Laredo public was said to be filling the theatre and "for the first time in many years in Laredo, we have seen the theatre filling with an attendance of intelligent people who have manifested in every way its satisfaction of the exquisite work that is offered to them" by the dramatic company performing there. Thus the performances were intended to provide moral instruction and the audiences were perceived as capable of comprehending that instruction and receptive of it as well.[11]

Many newspaper accounts show the relationship between the audience and the performers. It was through the benefit performances that the townspeople could best display their satisfaction with and gratitude toward the performers. At benefit perfor- mances audiences often gave the actors gifts, such as those given to Manuel Cotera at his benefit in San Antonio: a tie, vest, jacket hanger, box for collars, soaps, silver goblet, socks, cuff-links, and shirts. The theatre manager, Lucchese, was one of the few who gave him money. Most of the gifts were from married couples, al- though some were from young women. Many were from newspa- per men, actors and actresses residing in the city, and well-known people of the community. Of course, the reverse is true of benefit gifts to actresses, when gentlemen of the city showered special to- kens of their appreciation on them.

There are only two accounts of audience misbehavior. In the earlier account, the Laredo public was censured for permitting some audience members to shout and whistle at dramatic perfor- mances as well as concerts and other sorts of diversions:

> It is a shame for Laredo that at dramatic functions, concerts, and in general, all types of diversions, there are some individuals so ignorant and uneducated that they still manifest their enthusiasm and emotions with shouts and whis- tles that often reach the point of scandal.
>
> This type of enthusiastic display should not be permitted in any cultured [the word also means mannered] city and it is a display by the poorly edu- cated of Laredo and an affront to our society and forcibly calls the attention of the police.[12]

In the later account, the audience was scolded for applauding dur- ing the performance, interrupting the scene and thereby drawing away from the seriousness of the drama. The account was harsh, stating that "it is desired that the public not give such displays which are lacking in manners," for in order to praise the artist for his work there is "plenty of time for that" at the end of the scene.[13]

In general, the newspaper reviewers censured people severely if they failed to attend the benefits or to give sufficient applause after performances. In the account of 26 April 1916, the reporter wrote:

> One can consider it a patriotic duty and for the solidarity of our race to attend the artistic evenings offered by the Teatro Juárez [in San Antonio] where a modest group of Mexican actors [the Compañía María del Carmen Martínez] fight for their life in foreign soil. . . . It is necessary to attend the functions at the Juárez as often as possible where for a few cents one can reap the benefits . . . of drama. . . .[14]

The overall conclusions that may be drawn about audiences must be based on the plays they enjoyed. We know that the plays were of the following types: (1) those of highly emotional and melodramatic intensity showing actors deeply involved with their characters; (2) lengthy dramas of didactic and moralistic content which provoked thought and concern; (3) comic afterpieces which, although light and brief, were also didactic and moralistic; (4) plays based on familiar situations and themes from the Mexican past or about their ancestors' way of life; and (5) plays with abundant spectacle and elegance in production.

In such plays, there were both intellectually stimulating and emotionally entertaining aspects. The actors displayed their intelligence through comprehension of their roles and by knowing all of their lines; instruction by the dramatic companies was provided for audiences from a broad spectrum of society through both serious drama and comic afterpieces; the evening was filled with suitable entertainment for the entire family; and the plays made use of both formal and informal Spanish. From this we find that Mexican American audiences were both similar to and different from Anglo American audiences of the period.

Both audiences enjoyed realism in performances, wanted to be entertained, and were drawn to elaborate productions. The primary differences are the Mexican American audience's preference for traditional themes and ideas, rooted in the past and reflecting an idealized setting and a language that established associations with family and national past. The Mexican American audiences were quickly attracted to contemporary themes once companies began bringing the new drama to Texas.

Although films were always intriguing, they did not surpass theatrical activity in popularity until after 1930. Films were often offered jointly with plays and shown between dramatic performances or during the afternoon, but they were used especially to fill theatres when no theatrical companies were available to produce dramas. More importantly, it was not until about 1920 that Spanish-language films of good quality and featured stars were available in Texas.

Thus, the theatre provided the Mexican American with a type of entertainment that unified the community through language, themes based on familiar experiences and their history, fulfilled their sense of nationalism through identity with the mother country, and through entertainment suitable for the entire family. On an even broader base, however, we can see that Spanish-language professional dramatic companies brought a wide spectrum of society to the theatre.

Notes

1. Ricardo Romo,"The Urbanization of Southwestern Chicanos in the Early Twentieth Century," *New Scholar* 6 (1977): 183-207; Arnoldo De León, *The Tejano Community, 1836-1900* (Albuquerque: University of New Mexico Press, 1982).

2. Romo 194; U.S. Bureau of the Census, *Fifteenth Census of the U.S.: 1930 Population* (Washington, D.C., 1932) I: Table 23.

3. Carey McWilliams, *North From Mexico* (New York: Greenwood Press, 1968) 87.

4. *El Demócrata Fronterizo*, Laredo 4 July 1905: 4.

5. Manuel Gamio, *Mexican Immigration in the United States* (Chicago: University of Chicago Press, 1930); Romo 197-198.

6. *Evolución*, Laredo 22 December 1917: 2; *La Patria*, El Paso 15 July 1920; *Evolución* 15 August 1918.

7. *El Demócrata Fronterizo* 26 April 1916: 6; 11 May 1907: 2; *La Prensa*, San Antonio 19 May 1916: 5.

8. *El Demócrata Fronterizo* 10 December 1904: 4; 28 January 1905: 4; 29 April 1905: 4; 21 April 1906: 4.

9. *La Prensa* 12 May 1916: 5; 14 May 1915: 1.

10. *La Prensa* 10 February 1918: 5; 25 June 1917: 1; 12 May 1916: 5; 30 January 1918: 5.

11. *El Demócrata Fronterizo* 12 October 1907: 2, 4.

12. *El Demócrata Fronterizo* 5 January 1907: 5.

13.   *La Prensa* 9 November 1917: 5.

14.   *La Prensa* 26 April 1916: 6; 19 May 1916: 5.

Chapter VI

The Decline of Professional Dramatic Spanish-Language Companies in Texas

Several studies show that theatrical activity was a vibrant part of the developing cultural life in Texas. The Anglo American theatre, however, was dominated by large touring companies from the East Coast or abroad; such companies generally gave only one or two performances in each town they visited. In Texas, only the Mexican American community had professional theatre available to it on a regular basis.

Amateur Mexican American theatre in the United States has been traced back to the sixteenth century, yet the Spanish-language professional theatre in the United States is still little understood because information regarding its development is sadly lacking. We know that by the late nineteenth century, professional acting companies from Mexico were performing in Texas and that they helped to establish a lasting tradition in Texas and the United States. Although some research about these companies has been done, little scholarship on the development of the Spanish-language theatre in the southwestern states exists. It has been the intent here to investigate one part of the Mexican American theatre in the southwest--that in the State of Texas.

This study is a detailed account in English of the Mexican American stage and reflects a significant aspect of Mexican American culture in Texas. It shows, first, that alongside an amateur theatre, a professional theatre developed as companies came regularly to Texas from Mexico between 1875 and 1935; second, the values, beliefs, and aspirations which are apparent in representative plays produced by the professional dramatic companies, reflecting the culture and tastes of Mexican Americans; third, that three types of companies (touring, resident, and combination) appeared regularly and that each type used a distinct form of organization and operation; and fourth, that the theatre served as a cohesive force in the Mexican American community through language, themes, and intense performances intended for the entire family. Probably the single most significant discovery has been that Spanish-language theatrical activity appealed to such a wide spectrum of society that it created a firm cultural center which continued long after acting troupes disappeared.

The cross-cultural currents evident in Spanish-language theatre on the American stage reflect a broad exchange on both the Mexican and Texas communities and probably elsewhere in the United States. Through the performances the audiences became acquainted with the dramas, from the old and established plays to the modern repertory, both building and influencing the cultural life in America.

By the 1930's the larger cities of San Antonio, Laredo, and El Paso were firmly established theatrical centers in Texas for the Spanish-speaking community. It was, however, about this time that a noticeable decline of activity by the professional dramatic Spanish-language companies became evident. The dramatic touring companies had virtually ceased appearing in Texas by 1935, and this can be attributable to several factors. There was a change in the demand of the audiences for the newer, more popular forms of entertainment such as the variety and comic entertainment and especially vaudeville. Mexico had begun exporting motion pictures in Spanish and Hollywood was also making such films featuring Mexican and Mexican American stars. These films were less expensive for an evening's entertainment both for the audience and the theatre management, thus making them a better commodity in each theatre.

Other factors certainly contributed to the demise of Spanish-language dramatic activity. Many of the older generation of performers began retiring, leaving the younger generation to follow the more popular new forms of entertainment both in the

United States and Mexico, that is, variety entertainment, film, and later, radio. Sra. Villalongín de Santos and Sr. Astol comment frequently on the many descendants of former company members that continued to perform in these media, such as those of the Padilla family once of San Antonio. Additional causes that probably contributed to the changing nature of Spanish-language theatrical entertainment in Texas are those of an increasing use of English and interest in English-language film and entertainment already evident in the changing language and society that preferred the comic short pieces that evolved into the sketches, revues, and vaudeville popular in the 30s. The single most important fact, nevertheless, lies in the serious economic instability that the United States faced in the 1930s. As Jack Poggi points out in *Theatre in America: The Impact of Economic Forces, 1870-1967*, the depression affected all acting companies and caused the decline of most. The situation was no different for the Spanish-language touring companies. The touring was costly and elaborate spectacles once so popular became impossible to finance with the increase of production and operation costs. Also, deportation and repatriation to Mexico were widespread. These events certainly would have caused a break in the flow of Mexican companies travelling across the border with the ease they had been accustomed to in the past.[1]

It is beyond the scope of this study to go further in investigating the activity of the professional dramatic companies of the Mexican American stage in Texas. It is not improbable that other companies existed which have not been documented here. It will require further research, however, before a definitive study on the entire spectrum of the Spanish-language professional dramatic companies that appeared in Texas can be complete. However, clearly by 1935, the major movement of Spanish-language theatre on the American stage was largely over, a period which witnessed the establishment of a theatrical tradition in the Spanish language and introduced audiences to innovative theatre and drama, providing continuing cultural entertainment for a long time in Texas.

Mexican American theatre thrived for about fifty years in Texas. Although it died out in the 1930s, the tradition was revived again in the 1960s. In the early twentieth century it appealed to a broad spectrum of the community; now it addresses itself to a very small portion of the Mexican American population. The reasons for this change are several. One factor is acculturation, for as the people became part of the mainstream, dominant society, their needs and desires changed. Yet even today there is a distinct Mexican American culture--not quite Mexican, not quite Anglo. Not all persons of Mexican heritage adhere to acculturation and some have vigorously resisted it. Mexican immigrants value the Spanish language and their ethnicity, and the intellectual culture of Mexico has continued to influence Mexican Americans. To this community language continues to be a prominent factor in the appeal of Mexican American theatre. Yet, film, radio and television began to supplement what had once been a restricted supply of entertainment; with the coming of radio and television the families could remain at home rather than go to the theatre. Also, the family was no longer as dominant as it once was, and identification with Mexico or Spain declined as other cultures and traditions began to influence the Mexican American community.

The most evident vestiges that remain from the era of great theatrical activity are the cultural centers which the dramatic troupes helped to establish. These centers still exist today, thus providing evidence of the cohesiveness brought by this theatre, even as cultures are becoming more enmeshed. The cities are at once bilingual and multicultural. Immigrants from Mexico are drawn to those centers where their language, customs, and similarity of social class and ethnic characteristics exist. They bring their own folk culture, but at the same time adopt the customs, mores, and standards of the Chicano along with that of the dominant society they find in the United States.

As long as immigration continues from Mexico to the United States, there will be a group which Spanish-language dramatic activity can attract. In his study on "The Urbanization of Southwestern Chicanos," Ricardo Romo points out that the Chicano population today is the fastest growing group in the nation, already constituting the largest ethnic minority in the Southwest. He states: "In

California, for instance, the Mexican population has grown by more than a million in the last seven years, to a total of 4.2 million," and that "as an ethnic group, Chicanos are distinct in that 90 percent of their nearly 10 million members live in the Southwest." Records show that immigration has been continual since the 1930s. As long as this pattern continues, and there is little doubt that it will, there will be a demand for Spanish-language cultural activity. Rodolfo Acuña, in *Occupied America: A History of Chicanos* states that "cultural identity played a major role in unifying Chicanos of diverse urban centers of the Midwest." One would assume the same would be true of the Southwest as well.[2]

Further scholarship must still be devoted to Mexican American theatre. We need even more information than has been gathered here from the remaining participants in pre-World War II Texas theatre and those from parts of the Southwest other than Texas.

The revived Mexican American theatre did not come into prominence until 1965 with the founding of El Teatro Campesino; the success of that company gave rise to a whole generation of Chicano theatre groups. Luis Valdez, the director of El Teatro Campesino, has been credited with illuminating the cultural tradition of Mexicans living in the United States by using his art to relate this tradition to society as a whole. Valdez and other Chicano dramatists have looked to pre-Columbian ritual and ceremonies along with the amateur dramatic tradition as the primary source from which Spanish-language theatre stemmed. The present study provides another link in the long tradition of Mexican American theatre. Contemporary groups should benefit from knowledge of this dramatic heritage that was so prominent in Texas, making a valuable contribution to the annals of American theatre history.

Notes

1. Jack Poggi, *Theatre in America: The Impact of Economic Forces, 1870-1967* (Ithaca, New York: Cornell University Press, 1968) 65-96.

2. Ricardo Romo, "The Urbanization of Southwestern Chicanos in the Early Twentieth Century," *New Scholar* 6 (1977) 183; "Census: City has Highest Hispanic Percentage," *The San Antonio Light* 26 March 1982: 20-D; Rodolfo Acuña, *Occupied America: A History of Chicanos*, 2nd ed. (New York: Harper and Row, Publs., 1980) 299-342, 350-351; Carey McWilliams, *North From Mexico* (New York: Greenwood Press, 1968) 209-217, 290.

Appendix I

Broadsides Used by Compañía Carlos Villalongín

Broadside announcing performance of *Tierra Baja*, place and date unknown but known to be prior to arrival in San Antonio (before 1911) while still in Mexico.

Two broadsides announcing events at Teatro Aurora, 1911, San Antonio, Texas.

Broadside announcing event at Teatro Salón San Fernando, 23 October 1915, San Antonio, Texas.

TEATRO.

COMPAÑIA CÓMICO DRAMÁTICA CARLOS VILLALONGIN.

¡GRAN FUNCION PARA HOY!

DEBUT de la Compañía con la hermosa producción dramática de los tiempos modernos, de gran éxito en todos los teatros del mundo

TIERRA BAJA

NOCHE DE GALA! No hay más allá!

AL PUBLICO. Atendiendo á la delicadeza y buen gusto literario del distinguido auditorio que nos honra, llevamos hoy al palco escénico la inimitable obra TIERRA BAJA, la que habiendo sido traducida á los principales idiomas del mundo, ha constituido siempre un gran acontecimiento. Nosotros estamos verdaderamente seguros de que esta joya dramática será del agrado del inteligente público que nos favorezca, pues es uno de los más legítimos triunfos de la literatura española, delicadamente estudiada y puesta en escena por esta corporación, que no tiene más afán que el de que el auditorio quede contento.

LA COMPAÑIA.

PROGRAMA.

1º Obertura.
2º Representación del sublime drama dividido en tres actos, escrito en catalán por el distinguido dramaturgo D. Angel Guimerá, y traducido al español por el famosísimo dramaturgo D. José Echegaray, titulado:

¡TIERRA BAJA!

Reparto

MARTA.... SRITA. CONCEPCION HERNANDEZ.
Nuri...... Niña Dolores Magaña.
Antonia.... Srita. Herminia Villalongin.
Pepa...... Sra. Margarita Pérez.
MANELICH.... SR. CARLOS VILLALONGIN.
Sebastián.... Sr. Luis Hernández.
El Ermitaño.... Sr. Antonio Saldivar.
Morucho.... Sr. Levy C.
Nando.... Sr. Villalongin M.
José......
Mosén.... Sr. Alberto Orozco.
Peluca.... Sr. Cabrera D.

3º Por final la preciosa pieza en un acto, titulada:

L. N. B.

PRECIOS. ENTRADA GENERAL 30 CVS.

Muy pronto las grandes obras: Las dos Huérfanas, Los Pobres de México, La Mujer Adúltera, y la gran obra de D. Manuel Muriquiz Blanco, ALMAS RUSTICAS.

TEATRO AURORA

EMPRESA ∮ B. NORIEGA

2 FUNCIONES 2

Extraordinarias para la noche del

Sabado 30 DE Sept. 1911 · Domingo 1o DE Oct. 1911.

ESTRENO! ESTRENO!

Por primera vez en esta ciudad el monumental drama en 7 actos,
joya del Teatro Frances, que lleva por titulo:

LA ABADIA DE CASTRO

Los tres primeros actos tendrán verificativo El Sabado.   Los 4 restantes El Domingo.

AL PUBLICO   Una vez más doy á conocer cuanto estimo y cuan agradecido estoy por las deferencias de que he sido objeto por parte de las distinguidas familias que cariñosas acuden siempre á mi llamamiento. La obra que hoy tengo el gusto de anunciar es de aquellas cuyo recuerdo perdura siempre. Llena de moralidad, sublime y apasionada hasta el delirio, es un tesoro que guarda en sí saludables enseñanzas. Sin temor á duda, puedo asegurar que JAMAS se ha puesto en esta ciudad una obra de la índole de esta. Convencido estoy que ella hará época en los anales de este teatro.   LA EMPRESA

⟶ PROGRAMA ⟶

Escogidas vistas Cinematográficas.

Representación del famoso drama del celebre Bouchardy, que lleva por título:

SIXTO V o LA ABADIA de CASTRO

REPARTO

Elena .... Srita. C. Hernández	Rodolfo Ramuelo .... Sr. C. Villalongin	Hugo (Braht) .... Sr. A. Orozco
La Condesa .... Sra. M. Fernández	Julio Brachoderte .... Sr. L. Hernández	Mario .... Sr. F. Berrones Jr.
Sor Maria ...... Sra. H. de Villalongin	Cardenal Montalto .... Sr. A. Saldivar	Carini ....
La superiora .... Sra. A. Pineda	Conde de Campomala .... Sr. A. Orozco	Stiffano .... Sr. P. Valverde
La Tornera ...... Srita. M. Berrones	Fabio de Campomala,	Prior de Monte Cavi.	
Margarita .... Sra. A. Pineda	Gobernador de Roma. } .... Sr. J. Calderón	Serotii .... } Sr. C. Berrones Sr

LOS INTERMEDIOS SERAN CUBIERTOS POR LA ORQUESTA QUE DIRIJE EL PROFESOR SR. BOBADILLA.

⟶⟶ TITULO DE LOS ACTOS ⟵⟵

1o.   EL CASADOR.   2o.   El Consejo de Familia.   3o.   EL DESAFIO.
4o.   El Convento del Ave Maria   5o.   EL CUERPO DE BRAVIS.   6o.   Capilla Expiatoria.   7o.   SIXTO V.

Entrada   10c   ☞ No hay media paga

EN ESTUDIO   El Jorobado ó Enrique Lagardére y El Tenorio
Maderista.

IMPRENTA 415 Zavala St. MENDOZA PRINTING CO.

Appendix II

Examples of Companies' Repertory: List of Promptbook Titles not Previously Published

The form and method used here follows that used by John W. Brokaw in his article on "The Repertory of a Mexican-American Theatrical Troupe: 1849-1925," published in the *Latin American Theatre Review*. The list of promptbooks is organized alphabetically by the authors' last name. Each entry is divided into five sections, although not all may have sufficient information. The five sections are: (1) author's name; (2) the title of the play; (3) the date of the promptbook; (4) the genre and length of the play; and (5) additional information about the document such as details of previous owners of the document, cast lists, or the type of script, as for example, manuscript (ms).

The term *comedia* is retained where it has been specified rather than using the English translation "comedy" as Brokaw does since the term does not necessarily indicate that it is of a comic nature, but all other form and method remain similar.

The repertories are divided by individual collections. There are three known extant collections, namely, the Carlos Villalongín Collection and the Latin American Library Collection at The University of Texas at Austin; and the private collection of Sra. Otila Garza of Austin, Texas. The private collection of Sra. María Luisa Villalongín de Santos includes plays which are available in the Carlos Villalongín Collection.

The list of promptbooks in these collections is complete except for those of the Carlos Villalongín Collection which only includes those promptbooks not included in the list already compiled by John W. Brokaw.

Promptbooks of Plays found in the Lalo Astol Collection

Anonymous. #15. *La galana*, n.d., 3 act drama in prose.

Alonso Gómez, Sebastián with Manzano Mancebo, Luis. #61. *Lo que no muere*, n.d., 2 act *comedia*.

Álvarez Quintero, Serafín and Joaquín. #28. *El amor que pasa*, 1904, 2 act *comedia*.

Álvarez Quintero, Serafín and Joaquín. #61. *La media naranja*, 1894, one act comic afterpiece in prose.

Arniches, Carlos. #28. *La casa de Quirós*, 1915, 2 act comic farce. (There is an addition at the end of the play in the handwriting of Leonardo F. García.)

Arniches, Carlos. #10. *Me casó mi madre o las veleidades de Elena*, 1927, 3 act comic afterpiece.

Aza, Vital. #61. *El sueño dorado*, 1895, one act *comedia* in prose.

Bataille, Henry, Trans. to the Spanish by López Barbadillo, Joaquín and Tusquets, Enrique. #56. *La virgen loca*, 1915, 4 act drama.

Benavente, Jacinto. #55. *El nido ajeno*, 1894, 3 act *comedia* in prose.

Cano y Masas, Leopoldo. #55. *Mater dolorosa*, 1904, 3 act drama in prose.

Fernández Ardavin, Luis. #12. *Via crucis*, 1928, 3 act drama with prologue and epilogue in verse and prose.

Fernández del Villar, José. *¡Te la debo, Santa Rita!*, 1914, *entremes*.

Jardiel Poncela, Enrique. #52. *Una noche de primavera sin sueño*, 1927, 3 act humorous *comedia*.

Juan Diana, D. Manuel. #61. *Receta contra las suegras*, 1908, 1 act *comedia*.

Linares Rivas, Manuel. #26. *Frente a la vida*, 1920, 3 act *comedia* in prose.

Linares Rivas, Manuel. #36. *La mala ley*, 1923, 3 act *comedia*.

Linares Rivas, Manuel. #33. *Lo pasado o concluido o guardado*, 1922, 2 act *comedia*.

Linares Rivas, Manuel. #36. *Primero, vivir . . .* , 1923, 3 act *comedia*.

Martínez Sierra, Gregorio. #29. *Amanecer*, 1915, 3 act *comedia*.

Mendez Caldeira, Alfredo and Mario. #61. *Un drama extraño*, 1923, comic afterpiece in 2 scenes.

Millán Astray, Pilar. #15. *El juramento de la primorosa*, 1924, 3 act *sainete* in prose.

Muñoz Seca, Pedro. #5. *El alfiler*, 1929, 3 act *comedia*.

Muñoz Seca, Pedro. #3. *La bondad*, 1925, 3 act *comedia*.

Muñoz Seca, Pedro. #55. *La cartera del muerto*, 1920, 3 act serious drama in prose.

Muñoz Seca, Pedro. #3. *El espanto de Toledo*, 1926, 3 act "humorous drama" (*humorada*). (There is an addition on page 3 and at the end, the first typewritten and the second written in Leonardo F. García's handwriting.)

Muñoz Seca, Pedro. #16. *Lo que dos dispone*, 1925, 3 act *comedia*.

Muñoz Seca, Pedro with López Nuñez, Juan. #53. *El rayo*, 1917, 3 act comic afterpiece in prose.

Muñoz Seca, Pedro with Pérez Fernández, Pedro. #24. *El alma de Corcho*, 1931, 3 act comic afterpiece.

Muñoz Seca, Pedro with Pérez Fernández, Pedro. #42. *La cabalgata de los Reyes*, 1926, 3 act *comedia*.

Muñoz Seca, Pedro with Pérez Fernández, Pedro, #57. *Los campanilleras*, n.d., 3 act *comedia*.

Muñoz Seca, Pedro with Pérez Fernández, Pedro, #42. *Los extremenos [paralelos] se tocan*, n.d., operetta without music but with songs and overtures in 3 acts with prologue. (The title was changed from. "extremenos" to "paralelos," with the change handwritten.)

Muñoz Seca, Pedro with Pérez Fernández, Pedro. #57. *El sonámbulo*, 1925, 3 act comic afterpiece.

Paradas, Enrique with Jiménez, Joaquín. #32. *La canastilla*, n.d. 2 act comic afterpiece.

Paso, Antonio with Abati, Joaquín. #58. *El orgullo de Albacete*, 1913, 3 act comic afterpiece adapted from the French play *Loute* by Pierre Weber.

Paso, Antonio with Abati, Joaquín. *Mi querido Pepe*, 1915, 2 act comic afterpiece in prose.

Paso, Antonio with Del Toro, Ricardo G. #3. *¡Sueltate el pelo, Rosario!*, 1927, 3 act comic farce in prose. (There is a typewritten addition at the end of the last act.)

Rey, Miguel and Nougués, Pablo. #61. *Jarabe de Pico*, n.d., 2 act *comedia*.

Sassone, Felipe. #31. *¡Calla, Corazon!*, 1923, 5 act *comedia* in prose.

Suárez de Deza, Enrique. #47. *He entrado una mujer*, 1925, 3 act *comedia* with third act divided into four scenes.

Promptbooks of Plays found in the Private Collection of Sra. Otila Garza, Austin, Texas (These promptbooks were originally owned by her father, Lalo Astol, and previously by her grandfather, Leonardo F. García.)

Anonymous. *El sexo debil*, n.d., 2 act *comedia*. (MS includes cast list and stamp of Adela Hidalgo.)

Anonymous. *La llorona*, 1908, 4 act drama. (MS Copy of Margarita Fernández, Torreon, Coahuila, dated 23 October 1908. The author may be Francisco C. Neve who wrote the 1911 manuscript in the Carlos Villalongín Collection.)

lvarez Quintero, Serafín and Joaquín. *Mañana el sol*, n.d., comic paso. (MS See *María la emparedada* by Antonio García Gutiérrez.)

Echegaray, D. Miguel. *Champagñe frappé*, 1888, 1 act comic afterpiece in verse. (MS signed by Pascual Sánchez, Mexico.)

Echegaray, Miguel. *Echar la llave*, 1889, 1 act *comedia* in verse. (This printed text bears a stamp of the Compañía Cómico Dramática Española de José S. Paez and has the signature of the first prompter, Celaya A. Becerra.)

Garcia Gutiérrez, Antonio. *María la emparedada*, n.d., 4 act drama with prologue. (MS which includes the comic *paso Mañana el sol* by Serafín and Joaquín Álvarez Quintero. Property of Margarita Fernández, an actress that was a member of the Compañía José Martínez de la Lastra.)

Guimerá, Angel. *Tierra baja*, 1913, 3 act drama in prose. (This manuscript bears a stamp of the Archive of Victoria Sala, Monterrey, Mexico, 1913. It also has the signature of Juan Antonio Negrete and Janey Loper Bosh. Sra. Sala was the director of her own company in Mexico in 1909.)

de Larra, Luis with music by Maestro Fernández Caballero y Hermosa. *La trapera*, 1915, one act *zarzuela* with four scenes in prose and verse. (MS signed by F. Navarro in Morelia, Mexico.)

Liern, D. Rafael Maria. *Dos canarios de café*, 1911, 1 act comic *zarzuela* in prose. (MS bears a stamp which indicates that the archive and costumes are the property of Emilia Marti de González, dated 14 December 1911, Mexico with initials V. G. G.)

Lustonó, Eduardo, *Basta de suegros*, n.d., 1 act comedy in prose. (MS includes cast list. Copy is property of Margarita Fernández.)

Pina, D. Mariano. *La lluvia de oro*, 1888, 1 act comic afterpiece. (Property of Victoria Sala. Initials JAN also stamped on text.)

Promptbooks of Plays found in the Carlos Villalongín Collection Not Already Listed by John W. Brokaw in his Article on the Repertory of the Compañía Hernández-Villalongín

Anonymous. A. 23. *Los cuates vaciladores*, 1 act dialogue.

Anonymous. A. 24. *El grito de independencia*, n.d., drama in 3 scenes.

Escudero, Manuel and Espinosa, Francisco. A. 27. *El fin del mundo o el cometa de 1872*, 1872, 1 act comic afterpiece.

Gamboa, Frederico. A. 55. *Santa*, n.d., 4 act drama.

García, Leonardo F. A. 81. *Rosas de pasión*, adaptation of the original by S. Andres de Prado, 1917, 3 act *comedia* with a prologue. (Adapted for fewer actors than those required for the original drama by Leonardo F. García, Alice, Texas, 1930.

Gaspar, Don Enrique. *Lola*, n.d., 3 act serious drama in prose.

Gil y Zarate, Antonio. A. 57. *Matilde ó a un tiempo dama y esposa*, n.d., 4 act drama.

Padilla Juan B. *Ramona*, 1930, adapted from the film version, 3 act drama in prose. (Given to Carlos Villalongín by Juan B. Padilla, "author of this play." Copied in Piedras Negras, Coahuila, 22 November 1930.)

Paradas, Enrique and Jimenez, Joaquín. A. 71. *El nido del principal*, 1915, 1 act *sainete* with 4 scenes. (This prompt script bears the stamp of Amelia Calvó Velasco and the Compañía Azteca of Leonardo F. García.)

Suarez, Constancio. A. 85. *Al borde del abismo*, n.d., 3 act drama.

Valladares y Saavedra, Ramon. A. 86. *Como marido y como amante*, 1879, 1 act comic afterpiece in prose.

Appendix III

List of Spanish-language Companies that appeared in Texas between 1900 and 1935.

Type of Company: Resident--R   Genre in which Company performs:

Itinerant--I	Opera--O	Comic--Cm	Variety--V
Combination--C	Dramatic--D	Lyric--L	Light Drama--LD
	Zarzuela--Z	Operetta--Ot	Machinations--M

Company Name	Place and Years in Texas	Comments
Evangelina Adams I/D	Laredo, 1908	Although the newspaper article mentioned that the company was appearing in Saltillo, Mexico, the company was expected in Laredo.
Areu I/Z/D/C	El Paso, 1916	
Rosita Arriaga de Lara C/D	El Paso, 1920	
Automatas I/M	San Antonio, 1916	
Azteca I/D	Laredo, San Antonio, Texas Valley, 1925-1935	
Dramática Azteca I/D	Roma, c. 1915-1925	Mariano Villalongín performed with this company according to "Memoirs of Carlos Villalongín," p. 179; although dates and places are unknown at least the performance in Roma, Texas can be verified.
Alfonso Calvó I/D	Laredo, 1907	Monterrey, Mexico, 1907
Antonio del Castillo I/D/Cm/L	Laredo, San Antonio, 1918	
Enrique del Castillo I/D	Laredo, San Diego, 1904; Laredo, 1905; Laredo, 1906	This company performed in Laredo and San Diego and thereafter proceeded to Matamoros, Mexico. In 1906 they were invited to inaugurate a new theatre in Laredo.
Castillo, Mondragon, and Graziani C/O	San Antonio, Corpus Christi, El Paso, Laredo, 1919	
Caussade de Leon I/Ot/Z	Laredo, 1918; San Antonio, Laredo, 1919	Arturo García Pajujo and his wife were appearing with this company in 1919.
Manuel Cotera I/D	San Antonio, Laredo, 1917; San Antonio, 1923; San Antonio, Laredo, 1925	

Company Name	Place and Years in Texas	Comments
Mimi Derba and Maria Caballe C/Ot/Z	Laredo, 1918; El Paso, 1919	
Estrella R/Z	El Paso, 1920	This company was the resident company of the Teatro Estrella.
Virginia Fábregas C/D	San Antonio, Laredo, El Paso, 1917; Laredo, San Antonio, 1918; El Paso, Laredo, San Antonio, 1919; San Antonio, El Paso, 1923; San Antonio, El Paso, 1926; San Antonio, Laredo, 1928.	
Marcelino Flores I/D	McAllen, 1930	
Garcinetti I/V?	Laredo, 1907	Although it is uncertain, the company appears to perform variety.
Genaro Garza I/V?	Laredo, 1905	Although it is uncertain, the company appears to perform variety.
Matilde Gonzales I/V	Duval, Nueces, Cameron and Starr counties, 1908	This company performed in this area on a two-month tour.
Hector Gorjoux I/O/Z	Laredo, 1905 possibly	This company appeared in Monterrey, Mexico and in a newspaper account of Laredo was referred to as "our old friend" so possibly appeared in Laredo sometime before. The company had appeared in Monterrey in 1905.
Prudencia Griffel I/Z	Laredo, 1909	This company performed in Monterrey and San Luis Potosi, Mexico, 1908.
Adolfo Gutiérrez I/D/Z	Laredo, 1905, 1907	In the tour of 1907, the company travelled from Laredo to Coahuila rather than going further into Texas; this company dissolved in Torreon, Mexico, 1908.
Iglesias-Astudillo I/D/Z	Laredo, 1917	This company continued on to Coahuila after they appeared in Laredo.

Company Name	Place and Years in Texas	Comments
Internacional I/o	San Antonio, 1916	
Italiana I/o	Laredo, 1907	After the appearance in Laredo, the company performed in Nuevo Laredo, Mexico.
Juvenil San Antonio ?/b	San Antonio, 1915, 1916	It is unknown whether this company was resident or itinerant but the only accounts available refer to its work in San Antonio.
Labrada y Flores I/z	Laredo, San Antonio, 1904	The newspaper account about this company stated that it was "very well-known in the city" so it must have appeared prior to the earliest known date of 19 November 1904. It was known to have appeared in Matamoros, 21 June 1904; Monterrey, 29 October 1904. After the performance in Laredo, the company continued on to San Antonio. Thereafter the accounts available indicate that it appeared in Mexico until 1908 but there is no indication that the company returned to Texas.
Sres. Ruiz Marid y Colina I/z	Laredo, 1907	
María del Carmen Martínez I/b	San Antonio, El Paso, 1915, San Antonio, Brownsville, 1916, San Antonio, 1917; Brownsville, Laredo, 1918; El Paso, 1920	The earliest account about this company is of its appearance in Durango, Mexico in 1908 in which the company had 25 actors. In 1916, the company toured from San Antonio to Brownsville and again to San Antonio. Thereafter appeared in Hachita, New Mexico. In 1920 the company appeared in El Paso and thereafter in Douglas, Arizona. In 1921 they were performing in Juárez, Mexico, across from El Paso, but it is unknown whether they performed in El Paso.
Martinez-Escalera I/z/N	El Paso, 1919	
José Martínez de la Lastra I/D	Laredo, 1905-1908, 1913, 1914, 1918	

Company Name	Place and Years in Texas	Comments
Elisa de la Maza I/D	Laredo, 1908	After appearing in Laredo, the company continued on to Monterrey, Mexico.
Juan Mellado I/D	San Antonio, 1917	In a newspaper account the company was said to have appeared in Eagle Pass sometime prior to the San Antonio appearance. (*La Prensa*, San Antonio, 5 August 1917, p. 5.)
Ricardo Mutio C/D	San Antonio, 1917	
Adda Navarete I/O	El Paso, 1917	
Mercedes Navarro C/D	El Paso, 1919	
Lydia Otero I/Z	Laredo, 1907, 1908	In 1907 the company performed in Laredo and then returned to perform in Nuevo Laredo, Mexico; they did not seem to continue in Texas.
Juan B. Padilla R/D/Z	San Antonio, 1913 Laredo, 1918	This company was resident in San Antonio at least in 1913; there are no specific dates of when it ceased to be resident there but in 1918 it was touring in Laredo. Sr. Padilla did eventually return to Mexico according to Sra. María Luisa Villalongín de Santos.
Pajujo I/C/Z/D	San Antonio, 1914, 1915; Laredo, 1917	This company performed only light drama but specialized in *zarzuela* and comedy. It made an extended stay in San Antonio between 11 December 1914 and 15 March 1915. In 1917 it performed in Laredo and thereafter in Monterrey, Mexico.
Profesor Reynald I/V	El Paso, 1920	
Carlos Sánchez de Lara I/D	San Antonio, 1915	
Francisco E. Solórzano I/D	Laredo, 1904-1908; San Antonio, 1905; Laredo, 1910-1911	This company was an itinerant company until 1910 when it became resident in Laredo. It is unknown how long the company continued to work. Prior to 1910, the company toured continuously between Laredo, once at least as

Company Name	Place and Years in Texas	Comments
Solórzano (cont.)		far north as San Antonio, and the stages of Mexico City. Its principal genre was dramatic but often it performed <u>zarzuelas</u> as well.
Teatro Salon Lincoln R/D	Laredo, 1918	
Ricardo de la Vega I/D/Z/Ot	Laredo, 1906; San Antonio, 1914-1915; El Paso, 1915, 1918; San Antonio, 1918; Laredo, 1919; El Paso, 1921	This company was itinerant until 1915 when the director, Sr. Ricardo de la Vega, took up permanent residency in El Paso. Thereafter tours were primarily within the El Paso and Chihuahua, Mexico area.
Adelina Vehi C/Ot/Z	El Paso, 1921	
Carlos Villalongín R/D	San Antonio, 1900, 1910-1916; Brownsville, 1913; Elmendorf, 1916	Carlos Villalongín, director, often took the company on tour during the summer months. The dates specified are those in which the company was known to have appeared according to available accounts in newspapers. It is probable that other cities were included in the tours. Prior to 1910 the company was an itinerant company, but thereafter it was a resident company in San Antonio at least until 1916.

Bibliography

Primary Sources

1. Private collection of Sra. María Luisa Villalongín de Santos includes promptbooks, plays, broadsides, photographs, and other memorabilia of the Compañía Villalongín-Hernández. San Antonio, Texas.

2. "Memoirs of Carlos Villalongín." Private collection of Sra. María Luisa Villalongín de Santos. San Antonio, Texas.

3. "Memoirs of Lalo Astol." Mexican American Library Collection, Latin American Library at The University of Texas at Austin.

4. Program, "Homage to Lalo Astol." Teatro Alameda, San Antonio, October 1981.

5. Program of "New Teatro Nacional." In the collection of Sra. Belia Camargo, San Antonio, Texas.

6. Railroad maps. Texas Archives at Barker Texas History Collection, The University of Texas at Austin, for the years 1890, 1900, 1915, 1917.

7. Medina, Rafael, with Adams, Manuel. *El globo terraqueo*, 1904. Promptbook in the Villalongín Collection, Mexican American Library Collection, Latin American Library at The University of Texas at Austin.

8. Promptbooks in the Villalongín Collection, Mexican American Library Collection, Latin American Library at The University of Texas at Austin.

9. Promptbooks in the Lalo Astol Collection, Mexican American Library Collection, Latin American Library at The University of Texas at Austin.

10. Private collection of promptbooks, plays, and other memorabilia, Sra. Otila Garza, Austin, Texas.

Newspapers

Laredo Newspapers
El Boletín Fronterizo, 1930-1931.
El Correo de Laredo, 1891-1895.
La Crónica, 1910-1911, 1914.
El Demócrata Fronterizo, 1904-1919.
Evolución, 1917-1920.
El Horizonte, 1884.

San Antonio Newspapers
La Época, 1916-1931.
La Fe Católica, 1897-1900.
El Imparcial de Tejas, 1917-1921.
La Prensa, 1913-1956.

El Paso Newspapers
El Clarín del Norte, 1906.
El Paso del Norte, 1904, 1906, 1915.
La Patria, 1919-1920, 1921-1925.
La Reforma Social, 1912.
La República, 1919-1920.
Revista Católica, 1875-1962.

Brownsville Newspaper
El Cronista del Valle, 1924-1930.

San Diego Newspaper
El Horizonte, 1879-1880.

Eagle Pass Newspaper
Daily Guide or *International News Guide*, 1922-1938.

Corpus Christi Newspaper
El Paladín, 1929-1930-1931, 1933-1935.

Edinburg Newspaper
El Defensor, 1930.

Interviews

Personal Interviews
Sr. Lalo Astol, San Antonio, 19 May 1981.
Sra. Belia Camargo, San Antonio, 15 July 1981.
Sra. Otila Garza, Austin, Texas, May 1981.
Sr. Cano Lucchese, San Antonio, 19 May 1981.
Sra. Clementina Navarro, San Antonio, May 1981.
Sra. Margarita C. Ramírez, San Antonio, May 1981.
Sr. Pedro F. Ramírez, San Antonio, December 1981.
Sra. María Luisa Villalongín de Santos, San Antonio, 19 May 1981.

Telephone Interviews
Sr. Lalo Astol, November 1981.
Sra. María Luisa Villalongín de Santos, November 1981.

Secondary Sources

Acuña, Rodolfo, *Occupied America: A History of Chicanos*. 2d ed. New York: Harper and Row, Publishers, 1981.

lvarez Quintero, Serafín and Joaquín. *El genio alegre*. 2d ed. Madrid: Sociedad de Autores Españoles, 1908.

Brockett, Oscar G. *History of the Theatre*. 3d ed. Boston: Allyn and Bacon, Inc., 1977, 5th ed., 1987.

Brockett, Oscar G. *The Theatre: An Introduction*. 3d ed. New York: Holt, Rinehart and Winston, Inc., 1974.

Bueno, Manuel. *Teatro español contemporaneo.* Madrid: Biblioteca Renascimiento, 1909.

Carilla, Emilio. *El romanticismo en la América Hispánica*. Madrid: Editorial Gredos, 1975.

Cejador y Frauca, D. Julio. *Historia de la lengua y literatura castellana*. Madrid: Tipográfica de la "Revista de Archivos Bibl. y Museos, 1917. VII.

Chandler, Richard E. *A New History of Spanish Literature.* Baton Rouge: Louisiana State University Press, 1961.

Danchert Castillo, María Estella. *Ignacio Rodríguez Galván y su obra*. Mexico City: Tipográfica Ortega, Universidad Nacional Autonoma de México, 1956.

Dehesa y Gómez Farías, María Teresa, *Introdución a la obra dramática de José Joaquín Fernández de Lizardi*. Mexico City: Universidad Nacional Autonoma de Mexico, 1961.

Deleito y Pinuela, José. *Origen y apogeo del "género chico."* Madrid: Revista de Occidente, 1949.

De Leon, Arnoldo, *The Tejano Community*. Albuquerque: U. of New Mexico Press 1973.

Dublan y Compañía, ed. *Obras dramáticas de José Peón Contreras,* Mexico City: Imprenta del Comercio, De Dublan y Comp., 1879.

Echegaray, José, trans. *Tierra baja*. By Angel Guimerá. 2d ed. Madrid: R. Velasco, Imprenta, 1900.

Gamio, Manuel. *Mexican Immigration in the United States*. Chicago: U. of Chicago Press, 1930.

de la Guardia, Alfredo. *El teatro contemporaneo*. Buenos Aires: Editorial Schapire, 1945.

"Historical Background on Seven Downtown Theatres in San Antonio, Texas." Unpublished research compiled by San Antonio Conservation Society and Arts Council of San Antonio, June 1978.

The Institute of Texan Cultures, San Antonio: The University of Texas at San Antonio, 1970-1979.

Jones, Willis Knapp. *Behind Spanish American Footlights*. Austin: University of Texas Press, 1966.

Kilgarriff, Michael. *The Golden Age of Melodrama*. London: Wolfe Publishing Limited, 1974.

McWilliams, Carey. *North From Mexico*. New York: Greenwood Press, Publishers, 1968.

Magaña-Esquivel, Antonio. *Breve historia del teatro Mexicano*. Mexico City: Ediciones de Andrea, 1958.

Mañon, Manuel. *Historia del Teatro Principal de México*. Mexico: Editorial "Cultura," 1932.

Marín, Diego. *La civilización española*. New York: Holt, Rinehart and Winston, Inc., 1961.

Metz, Leon C. *City at the Pass: An Illustrated History of El Paso*. California: Windsor Publications, Inc., 1980.

Miller, Jordan Y. *American Dramatic Literature*. New York: McGraw-Hill Co., 1961.

Monterde, Francisco. *Bibliografía del teatro en México*. New York: Burt Franklin, 1970.

Monterde, Francisco, ed. *Fernando Calderón: Dramas y poesías*. Mexico City: Editorial Porrua, S.A., 1959.

Olavarría y Ferrari, Enrique de. *Reseña historical del teatro en México: 1538-1911*. Mexico City: Editorial Porrua, S.A., 1961.

Paredes, Americo. *A Texas Mexican Cancionero*. Urbana: University of Illinois Press, 1976.

Poggi, Jack. *Theatre in America: The Impact of Economic Forces, 1870-1967*. Ithaca, N.Y.: Cornell University Press, 1968.

Quirk, Robert E. *Mexico*. New Jersey: Prentice-Hall, Inc., 1971.

Reyes de la Maza, Luis. *El cine Sonoro en México*. Mexico, 1973.

Reyes de la Maza, Luis. *El teatro en México*. Mexico: U.N.A.M., 1953-1970.

Shergold, N.D. *A History of the Spanish Stage from Medieval until the End of the Seventeenth Century*. Oxford: Clarendon Press. 1967.

Simpson, Leslie Byrd. *Many Mexicos*. Los Angeles: University of California Press, 1969.

Spell, Jefferson Rea. *Life and Works of José Joaquín Fernández de Lizardi*. Philadelphia: University of Pennsylvania, 1931.

Usigli, Rodolfo. *Mexico in the Theatre*. Trans. Wilder P. Scott. University of Mississippi: Romance Monographs, Inc., 1975.

U.S. Bureau of the Census, *Fifteenth Census of the U.S.: 1930 population* (Washington, D.C. 1932) I: Table 23.

Articles

Brady, Donald V. "The Theatre in Early El Paso: 1881-1905." *Southwestern Studies*, 4.1 (1966): 3-39.

Brokaw, John W. "A Mexican American Acting Company, 1849-1924." *Educational Theatre Journal* 27 (1975): 23-27.

Brokaw, John W. "Chicano Theatre: Some Reflections." *Educational Theatre Journal* 29, 4 (December 1977): 535-544.

Brokaw, John W. "A Nineteenth-Century Mexican Acting Company–Teatro de Iturbide: 1856-57." *Latin American Theatre Review* (Fall 1972): 23-30.

Brokaw, John W. "The Repertory of a Mexican-American Theatrical Troupe: 1849-1924." *Latin American Theatre Review* (Fall 1974): 25-35.

Huerta, Jorge A. "Chicano Agit-Prop: The Early Actos of El Teatro Campesino." *Latin American Theatre Review* 10 (1977): 45-48.

Huerta, Jorge A. "Chicano Teatro: A Background." *Aztlán* 2.2 (Fall 1971): 63-78.

Huerta, Jorge A. and Harrop, John. "The Agitprop Pilgrimage of Luis Valdez and El Teatro Campesino." *Theatre Quarterly* 5 (1975): 30-39.

Ramírez, Elizabeth C. "A History of Mexican American Professional Theatre in Texas Prior to 1900." *Theatre Survey* 24 (1983): 99-116.

Ramírez, Elizabeth C. "Compañia Juan B. Padilla." *American Theatre Companies: 1888-1930.* Ed. Weldon Durham. 3 vols. Connecticut: Greenwood Press, 1986: 353-358.

Ramírez, Elizabeth C. "Compañia Teatro Solórzano." *American Theatre Companies: 1888-1930.* Ed. Weldon Durham. 3 vols. Connecticut: Greenwood Press, 1986: 413-416.

Ramírez, Elizabeth C. "Compañia Villalongín." *American Theatre Companies: 1888-1930.* Ed. Weldon Durham. 3 vols. Connecticut: Greenwood Press, 1986: 449-453.

Ramírez, Elizabeth C. "Spanish-language Combination Companies on The American Stage: Organization & Practice in Texas, 1915-1935," *Theatre History Studies*, 1989.

Romo, Ricardo. "The Urbanization of Southwestern Chicanos in the Early Twentieth Century." *New Scholar* 6 (1977): 194.

Dissertations

Carvajal, Christa. "German Theatre in Central Texas." Diss. U. of Texas at Austin, 1977.

Huerta, Jorge A. "The Evolution of Chicano Theatre." Diss. U. of California at Santa Barbara, 1974.

Manry, Joe. "A History of the Theatre in Austin: 1839-1905." Diss. U. of Texas at Austin, 1979.

Myler, Charles B. "A History of the English-Speaking Theatre in San Antonio before 1900." Diss. U. of Texas at Austin, 1968.

Ramírez, Elizabeth C. "A History of Mexican American Professional Theatre in Texas: 1875-1935." Diss. U. of Texas at Austin, 1982.

Yoakum, Jack H. "A History of Theatre in Houston: 1836-1954." Diss. U. of Wisconsin at Madison, 1955.

Illustrations

ILLUSTRATION I. Child actress, María Luisa Villalongín, daughter of Carlos Villalongín, 1917 or 1918, San Antonio. In *Los granujas*, comic afterpiece. Photograph No. 1 in the Villalongín Collection. The University of Texas at Austin.

ILLUSTRATION II. Comic actress, Dolores Gamir, in role of old lady in *La viejecita*, comic afterpiece. This photo postcard was sent to Herminia Villalongín, 24 April 1924, San Antonio. Photo was printed in Nuevo Leon, Monterrey, Mexico. Photograph No. 19 in the Villalongín Collection. The University of Texas at Austin.

ILLUSTRATION III. Theatre Bulletin from Mexico, c. before 1911. Villalongín Collection. The University of Texas at Austin.

ILLUSTRATION IV. Manuel Cotera, leading actor; picture postcard typical of those sent to individuals, requesting that they sponsor the actor at his benefit performance; for benefit performance of Thursday, 11 March 1920, 8 p.m., Teatro Nacional, San Antonio. Photograph No. 5 in the Villalongín Collection. The University of Texas at Austin.

ILLUSTRATION V. A. de la Paz, actor, 12 February 1880, Laredo. Photograph No. 11 in the Villalongín Collection. The University of Texas at Austin.

ILLUSTRATION VI. Leonardo G. Astol [Lalo Astol] as young boy, probably in comic role, about 1915. Private collection of Sra. Otila Garza, Austin, Texas.

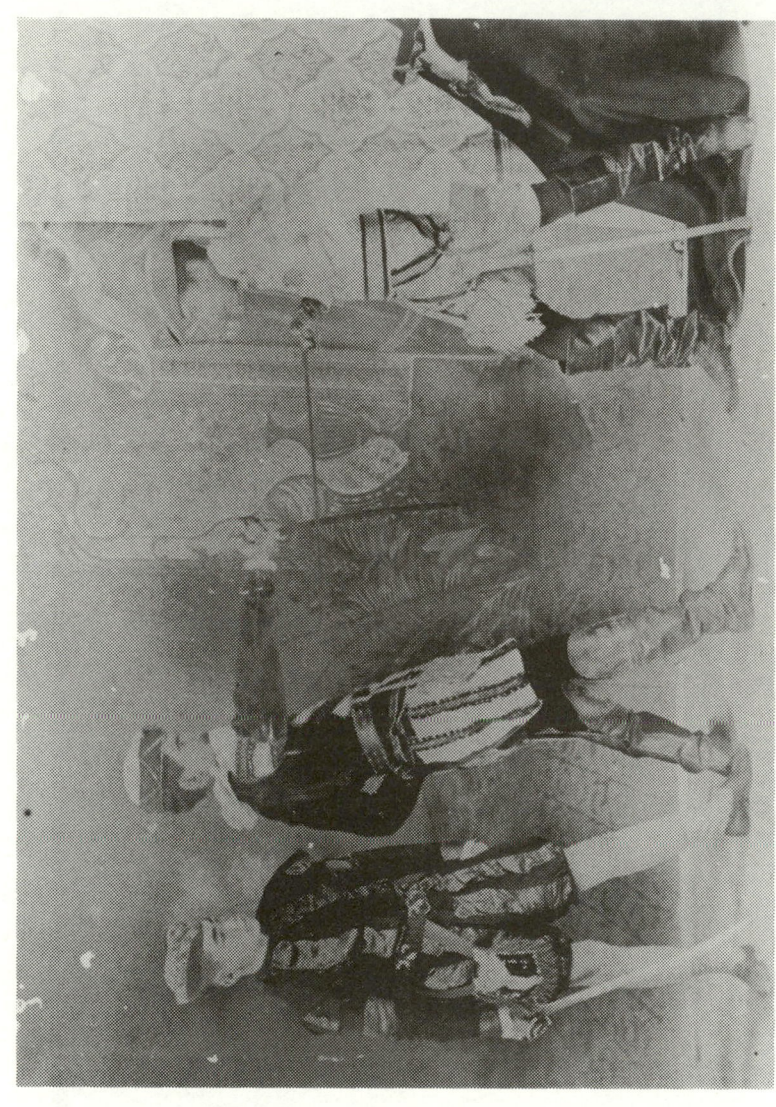

ILLUSTRATION VII. Young boys in period costumes. Photograph No. 25 in the Villalongín Collection. The University of Texas at Austin.

ILLUSTRATION VIII. Comic actors Mariano and Herminia Villalongín, brother and sister of Carlos Villalongín. c. 1900-1920. Photograph No. 27 in the Villalongín Collection. The University of Texas at Austin.

ILLUSTRATION IX. Antonia Pineda de Hernández, c. before 1911. Photograph
No. 30 in the Villalongín Collection.

ILLUSTRATION X. Concepción Hernández, leading actress with the Compañía Villalongín. Daughter of Encarnación and Antonio Pineda de Hernández. c. 1920. Photograph No. 29 in the Villalongín Collection. The University of Texas at Austin.

ILLUSTRATION XI. Carlos Villalongín, Empresario and leading actor, after 1911. San Antonio, Texas. Photograph No. 31 in the Villalongín Collection. The University of Texas at Austin.

ILLUSTRATION XII. Photo postcard for the benefit performance of Leonardo Astol [Lalo Astol] as young gallant (*galán joven*), about 15 years old, after 1920. Back of photo for the benefit performance of Leonardo Astol contains the following: "Would you do me the honor of sponsoring me in my benefit performance?" Private collection of Sra. Otila Garza, Austin, Texas.

Pajujo, el Beneficiado.

ILLUSTRATION XIII. Paid newspaper advertisement of benefit performance for Pajujo in Monterrey, Mexico, 12 December 1909, p. 1. The Villalongín Collection. The University of Texas at Austin.

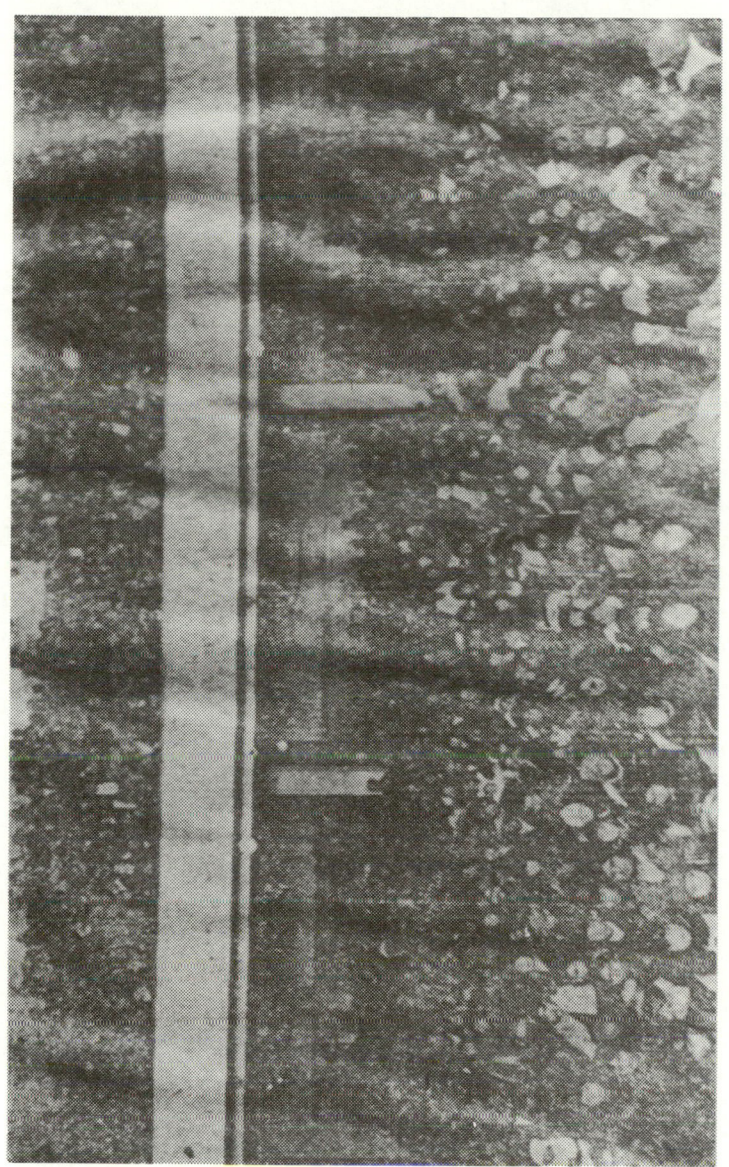

ILLUSTRATION XIV. Photograph of audience at Teatro Nacional, San Antonio, for a Christmas benefit. Note: people are seated in both the gallery and below. Only known extant photograph of theatre interior. *La Prensa*, San Antonio, 25 December 1924, front page.

Index

James C. Burge

LINES OF BUSINESS
Casting Practice and Policy in the American Theatre, 1752–1899

American University Studies: Series IX (History). Vol. 19
ISBN 0-8204-0312-1   307 pages   hardcover US $ 34.00*

*Recommended price – alterations reserved

The tradition of «lines of business» – the possession of a part by an actor – had its genesis on the English-speaking stage in Elizabethan times and was well established by the mid-eighteenth century. In this highly original study, James Burge investigates the use of «lines» in eight major American theatre companies. Burge sees in the impact of lines of business on the chief dramatic form of the nineteenth century – the melodrama – a demonstration of the power of this incipient trade unionism in casting and in the choice of repertory. With the rise of the director at the end of the century, lines of business ceased to be a controlling factor in casting practice and policy in the American theatre.

Contents: Development of casting policy and practice in the American theatre from 1752–1899 – Influence of the practices of the English-speaking stage of Elizabeth times and changes in American practice that came with the rise of the director in the theatre of the end of the eighteenth century.

PETER LANG PUBLISHING, INC.
62 West 45th Street
USA – New York, NY 10036